지옥

1

STORY
YEON SANG-HO

COVER & ART
CHOI GYU-SEOK

TRANSLATION
DANNY LIM

LETTERING
MICHAEL HEISLER

DARK HORSE BOOKS

THIS IMAGE WAS TAKEN THE MOMENT THE **NOTICE** TOOK PLACE IN THAILAND IN 2014.

THE AMOUNT OF TIME GIVEN TO THE RECIPIENT CAN VARY FROM THREE DAYS TO TWENTY YEARS.

DOESN'T MATTER WHERE THE RECIPIENT IS OR WHAT HE OR SHE DOES DURING THE ESTIMATED TIME PERIOD.

HELL'S **DEMONSTRATION** WILL BE CARRIED OUT...

DAMMNNNN LOOK AT THIS SCUFFED CG.

YOU GOT TO PUT IN AT LEAST A BIT OF EFFORT IF YOU WANT ME TO FALL FOR A SCAM LIKE THIS.

A LOT OF PEOPLE BELIEVE IT THESE DAYS. THERE'S TONS OF VIDEO EVIDENCE.

7

8

THIS GUY DOES A LOT OF GOOD THINGS TOO.

OKAY. OKAY.

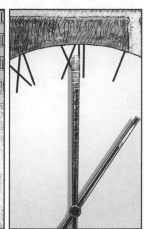

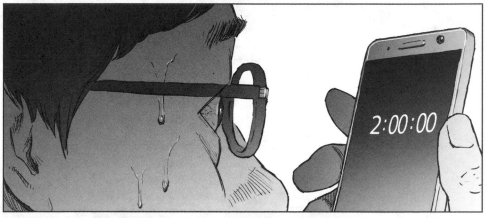

2:00:00

ヲ THUMP

ヲ THUD

ヲ THUMP

ヲ THUMP

ヲ THUMP

ヲ THUMP

ヲ THUMP

ヲ THUMP

ヲ O

THUMP

CRACK

AH...
UGH...

KYAH!

15

AH...PLEASE...

PLEASE...

UGH!
AHHH!

AH...!

AAHHH!

AAAAAHHHHHH!

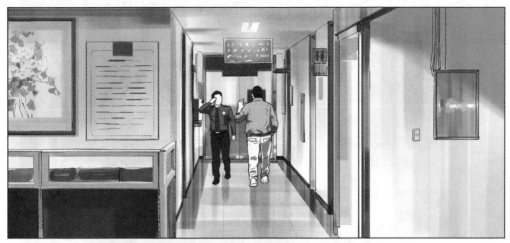

TIME OF THE INCIDENT: EXACTLY TWO O'CLOCK *PM*.

SUSPECT CAME IN BY BREAKING THE OUTER WALL AND WINDOWS OF THE CAFÉ...

WHEN DID THEY START?

JUST NOW. YOU CAME JUST IN TIME.

THE SPECIFIC METHOD OF HOMICIDE HASN'T BEEN REVEALED YET BUT...

...THE BODY SEEMS TO HAVE BEEN BURNT AT A VERY HIGH TEMPERATURE IN A SHORT DURATION OF TIME.

FROM THE RESULTS OF THE VICTIM'S VEHICLE INSPECTION:

YOUNG HOON JOO. FORTY-THREE YEARS OLD.

HE LIVED FIFTEEN MINUTES AWAY FROM THE CRIME SCENE.

AS FOR HIS BEREAVED FAMILY, HE HAD AN EX-WIFE THAT HE DIVORCED TWO YEARS AGO AND NO CHILDREN.

HAPSEONG STATION...HAPSEONG STATION MONSTER... HAPSEONG STATION MURDER...

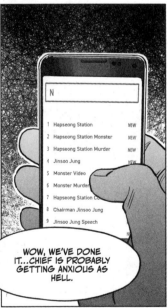

WOW, WE'VE DONE IT...CHIEF IS PROBABLY GETTING ANXIOUS AS HELL.

OH MY GOD! WHAT... WHAT IS THAT THING?!

THERE WERE TOO MANY EYEWITNESSES. VIDEOS RELATED TO THE INCIDENT ARE ALL OVER THE WEB.

HONEY, THE CAR... MOVE THE CAR... HURRY...

WHAT...

...ARE THOSE...?

6   Monster Murder

7   Hapseong Station Cult

8   Chairman Jinsoo Jung

9   Jinsoo Jung Speech

10   Jinsoo Jung New Truth

JINSOO JUNG? NEW TRUTH?

WHAT IS THIS?

23

WHAT ARE YOU LOOKING AT?

PHONE.

NEVER MIND.

NEW TRUTH SOCIETY IS A NEWLY RISEN RELIGION...

...THAT HAS BEEN EXPANDING ITS CONGREGATION THROUGH THE INTERNET IN RECENT YEARS.

THERE IS A CONCORDANCE BETWEEN ONE OF THE RELIGIOUS DOGMAS OF THE SAID RELIGION AND THE INCIDENT.

RUMORS SAY THAT IT IS SOME KIND OF A REVELATION FROM GOD AND IT IS RAPIDLY SPREADING ON THE INTERNET.

YOU HEAR THAT? YOU KNOW WHAT HAPPENS WHEN AN INCIDENT THAT HAS THE PUBLIC'S ATTENTION DRAGS ON, RIGHT?

LET'S CATCH THE SUSPECT BEFORE IT GETS NOISY, OKAY?

BUT IS THAT THING EVEN HUMAN?

CATCH HIM.

WHETHER HE'S HUMAN OR NOT, WE'LL FIND OUT ONCE WE INTERROGATE HIM.

WATCH YOUR MOUTH WHEN YOU TALK TO THE REPORTERS.

TEAM 1 WILL BE IN CHARGE OF THE VICTIM'S SURROUNDINGS. TEAM 2, INVESTIGATE THE CRIME SCENE.

KYUNG HOON AND EUN PYO.

YEAH?

THAT RELIGIOUS GROUP IS SUPPOSEDLY HAVING A GATHERING NEAR THE CRIME SCENE.

COULD BE AN ACT OF FANATICISM, BUT WHATEVER IT IS, IT SEEMS LIKE IT COULD BE ASSOCIATED WITH THE INCIDENT. YOU TWO GO LOOK INTO IT.

TRY NOT TO IRRITATE THEM.

IT'LL BE A PAIN IN THE ASS IF YOU RUB THEM THE WRONG WAY.

KYUNG HOON JIN.

25

DO YOU NOT WANT A PROMOTION?

I'M TRYING TO HELP YOU OUT HERE BUT YOU GOT TO AT LEAST ACT LIKE YOU WANT IT.

...?

JUST HURRY IT UP, YOU PUNK!

PEOPLE DIE WHEN THEY CHANGE.

UGH... THAT SLOW BASTARD...

NEW TRUTH SOCIETY.

A RELIGIOUS GROUP FOUNDED BY CHAIRMAN JINSOO JUNG IN 2012.

26

IT'S NOT THAT OLD. BEEN AROUND FOR ABOUT TEN YEARS.

THE PRECISE NUMBER OF FOLLOWERS ISN'T MENTIONED EITHER.

WHAT ARE YOU READING?

WIKIPEDIA.

THERE ARE SUSPICIONS THAT *ARROWHEAD* IS COMPOSED OF DEVOTED BELIEVERS OF THIS RELIGION.

ARROW-HEAD?

THOSE CRAZY BASTARDS THAT REVEAL THE IDENTITIES OF EX-CONVICTS ON THE INTERNET?

THAT'S THEM?

THEY CAUSE A LOT OF TROUBLE *IRL*, TOO.

ACCORDING TO CHAIRMAN JINSOO JUNG, GOD DEMANDS HUMANS TO BE RIGHTEOUS...

SO, UM... AN ANGEL-LIKE BEING WILL COME TO TELL YOU WHEN YOU WILL BE SENT TO HELL...

...IS WHAT IT SAYS?

27

HA! AN ANGEL? HELL?

THEN IS THIS A DIVINE PUNISHMENT...THAT KIND OF A THING?

IT SAYS IT'S A DEMONSTRATION OF HELL...

I GUESS IT'S A WARNING OF SOME SORT TO PEOPLE? SOMETHING LIKE THAT.

WHAT KIND OF RELIGION IS THIS DEPRESSING? MYSTERY OF THE HOLY SPIRIT, SALVATION OF THE SOUL, DON'T THEY HAVE THINGS LIKE THAT?

DAMN, SHOULD I JUST DROP EVERYTHING AND MAKE A RELIGION?

LOOKS LIKE IT'S SELLING NOT BECAUSE OF ITS RELIGIOUS DOGMA BUT BECAUSE OF THEIR VIDEO EVIDENCE.

KIDS NOWADAYS LEARN EVERYTHING FROM VIDEO CLIPS.

WELL...

WHETHER IT'S GOD OR SOMETHING ELSE, IT'D BE NICE IF IT WERE TRUE.

NICE? WHAT WOULD BE NICE?

BECAUSE EVEN IF WE ARREST THOSE SICK BASTARDS...

...THEY'LL GET RELEASED FOR INSUFFICIENT EVIDENCE, INSANITY DEFENSE, AND THINGS LIKE THAT.

BUT DAMN, THEY REALLY DID SHRED HIM TO BITS.

COPS CATCH CRIMINALS.

WHETHER THEY KILLED A BAD GUY OR AN INNOCENT PERSON...

...WHETHER THEY KILLED TO SAVE THE WORLD OR JUST TO HAVE FUN...WE CATCH WHOEVER COMMITTED A MURDER.

THAT'S OUR JOB.

ONLY UP TO THAT PART.

29

YOU HERE?

DID YOU FIND ANYTHING?

NOPE. AN EYEWITNESS SAID THERE WAS SALIVA, BUT...

CAN'T FIND ANYTHING. NOT EVEN A FOOTPRINT.

NEW TRUTH OR WHATEVER IS HAVING A GATHERING?

IS THAT WHAT I HEARD?

THERE'S A LOUD MIC SOUND COMING FROM THE FOUR-WAY INTERSECTION OVER THERE.

HE HAD A REPUTATION OF BEING A GOOD HARD-WORKING MAN.

HE RECEIVED THE NOTICE SAYING THAT HE WOULD BE SENT TO HELL IN FIVE HOURS.

AND THIS IS THE FOOTAGE FILMED EXACTLY FIVE HOURS AFTER HE RECEIVED IT.

HEY...ONE SECOND...

EXCUSE US.

ARGH!

AAAHH!

AAAAAHHHH!

A COUPLE OF DAYS LATER, THREE BODIES WERE FOUND BURIED IN HIS HOUSE.

THEY WERE THE VICTIMS IN MISSING PERSON CASES THAT EVEN THE POLICE HADN'T BEEN ABLE TO SOLVE.

THIS PHOTO IS FROM JAPAN, SEVEN YEARS AGO.

THIS PERSON HAD MULTIPLE CRIMINAL RECORDS OF ASSAULT AND FRAUDULENT ACTIVITIES.

THIS IS FROM SIX YEARS AGO IN NICARAGUA. CHILD KIDNAPPING AND MURDER.

ALL THE CORPSES THAT YOU SEE...

...WERE KILLED BY THE SAME METHOD YOU'VE JUST WITNESSED AND...

...EVERY ONE OF THEM WAS GUILTY.

DRUG MANUFACTURING, THEFT, FRAUD...

...RAPE, ARSON...

...

WHY DO PEOPLE SIN?

PEOPLE WHO SAY THEY DEVOTE THEIR LIVES TO OTHERS...

...PEOPLE WHO SAY THAT HUMAN BEINGS SET THE MORAL STANDARD... OFTEN SAY...

THEY GREW UP IN A BAD ENVIRONMENT...

...THERE IS A CONTRADICTION IN OUR SOCIAL STRUCTURE...

...THEY HAVE A MENTAL DEFICIENCY...

...THEY WERE DRUNK, THEY WERE HIGH ON DRUGS...

34

WHERE IS THE WORD *HUMAN* BEING USED IN ALL OF THESE PHRASES?

THESE PEOPLE TALK AS IF WE ARE JUST AN EMPTY POCKET THAT NEEDS TO BE FILLED WITH WORLDLY SUBSTANCES.

PEOPLE SIN BECAUSE THEY WANT TO SIN.

BY DENYING THAT FACT, HUMAN BEINGS LOST HUMILIATION, A SENSE OF GUILT, ATONEMENT, REPENTANCE.

AND THEY STILL CALL THIS A CIVILIZATION.

GOD IS SHOWING US AN IMAGE OF HELL...

...VERY BLUNTLY.

GOD'S INTENTIONS ARE VERY CLEAR.

YOU HAVE TO BE MORE RIGHTEOUS.

35

PLEASE TAKE CARE.

CHAIRMAN JINSOO JUNG?

AH, YES. IT'S YOUR FIRST TIME HERE?

UH, WE'RE THE POLICE. HERE...

YES, HELLO.

BUT WHAT BRINGS YOU OFFICERS HERE?

WE'RE CURRENTLY INVESTIGATING THE MURDER THAT OCCURRED EARLIER TODAY...

MURDER?

OH! THE *NOTICE* THAT HAPPENED TODAY?

AH...HA HA, THE POLICE EVEN INVESTIGATE AN ACT OF GOD.

WELL, I GUESS A MURDER IS A MURDER IN YOUR PERSPECTIVE...

SO WHAT CAN I HELP YOU WITH?

?

AREN'T YOU SUPPOSED TO BE AT THE ACADEMY? WHAT THE HELL ARE YOU DOING HERE?

HEY, SUNG HO. IT'S BEEN A WHILE!

HURRY UP AND GO HOME!

FINE, OKAY. I'M LEAVING.

YOU BETTER NOT GET SIDE-TRACKED. GO STRAIGHT HOME. UNDERSTAND?

I SAID, OKAY!

TAKE CARE, SUNG HO. THANKS FOR TODAY.

39

SO, YOU'RE SUNG HO'S DAD.

WHAT A COINCIDENCE, HA HA.

WHAT'S GOING ON? WHY IS MY SON HERE?

OH...WE'VE MET A COUPLE OF TIMES DURING VOLUNTEER WORK.

BUT I JUST FOUND OUT THAT HE WAS HERE TODAY.

IF IT MAKES YOU FEEL UNCOMFORTABLE, I'LL TRY TALKING TO HIM TO AVOID ANY TROUBLE BETWEEN THE TWO OF YOU.

SO ANYWAYS, WE'RE HERE TO ASK YOU SOME QUESTIONS REGARDING TODAY'S INCIDENT.

I HAVE AN INTERVIEW TO GET TO.

WOULD IT BE OKAY TO TALK ON MY WAY THERE?

AH, OF COURSE! WHATEVER'S THE EASIEST FOR YOU.

DO YOU ALWAYS GO ON FOOT LIKE THIS, CHAIRMAN?

YOU CAN JUST CALL ME BY MY NAME. YOU'RE NOT A MEMBER.

OUR CONGREGATION PROVIDED ME WITH A CAR BUT I PREFER TO USE THE SUBWAY.

I GUESS YOU GUYS IMAGINED ME TO BE A CULT LEADER OF SOME SORT.

I'M NOTHING LIKE THAT.

YOU CAN THINK OF NEW TRUTH SOCIETY AS A KIND OF STUDY GROUP.

I'VE HEARD PEOPLE SAY IT'S A RELIGIOUS GROUP?

A LOT OF PEOPLE THINK OF US THAT WAY.

BUT RELIGION IS ONLY SOMETHING THAT YOU NEED WHEN YOU ARE SEVERED FROM GOD.

YOU HOLD A MEMORIAL SERVICE FOR YOUR DECEASED ANCESTORS, NOT FOR THOSE THAT ARE ALIVE. CORRECT?

WE PURSUE GOD'S INTERVENTION AND ANALYZE HIS PURPOSE.

WE REALLY DON'T HAVE ANY ROOM FOR PRAYERS AND OFFERINGS.

WHEN DID YOU START HAVING THOSE BELIEFS?

BELIEFS? IT'S ALL FACTS BASED ON EXPERIENCE.

AND SOON...

...IT'S GOING TO BECOME A UNIVERSAL TRUTH.

I'M PRETTY FAMILIAR WITH RELIGION, SINCE I GREW UP IN A CATHOLIC ORPHANAGE.

HOLY SHIT, POG!

HEY, THEY'RE LOOKING AT US.

YOU KNOW HOW IT IS WHEN YOU ARE BORN A CATHOLIC. YOU HAVE TO TREAT CHURCH LIKE IT'S SCHOOL.

OH, MY!

OH, CHAIRMAN. PLEASE TAKE MY SEAT!

NO, NO. PLEASE SIT DOWN.

I ALWAYS WANTED TO DIE WHEN I GREW UP.

NO...I DIDN'T HAVE ANY INTEREST IN LIVING.

I WAITED UNTIL I TURNED TWENTY TO THINK ABOUT HOW I SHOULD DIE.

WHY TWENTY?

I DIDN'T WANT PEOPLE TO SEE MY DEAD BODY.

YOU KNOW YOU GET MONEY WHEN YOU LEAVE THE ORPHANAGE, RIGHT?

WHILE MY BROTHERS WERE SEARCHING FOR A SMALL ROOM WITH $5,000 IN HAND...

...I WENT TO A MEADOW.

"THERE THE VULTURES...

"...TAKE CARE OF THE CORPSE."

THAT PERSON WHO SAVED THE PREGNANT WOMAN AND THE BABY...

NO WONDER YOU LOOKED FAMILIAR!

WOW! YOU WERE THAT PERSON, MR. CHAIRMAN.

KYUNG HOON, YOU KNOW TOO, DON'T YOU?

THAT CRAZY BASTARD SET THE FIRE BECAUSE HE GOT CAUGHT IN AN AFFAIR. I UNDERSTAND THAT QUESTIONING PEOPLE IS PART OF YOUR JOB...

...BUT IT'S SURPRISING THAT YOU SEE ME AS SOMEONE THAT CAN BRING HARM TO OTHER PEOPLE. HA HA.

ARROWHEAD SEEMS LIKE THEY CAN.

HA...THOSE PEOPLE...

THERE ARE SOME WHO TWIST OUR WORDS.

IT'S A HASSLE FOR US TOO. THEY'RE NOT OUR MEMBERS.

AND THEY AREN'T THE TYPE OF PEOPLE THAT WILL LISTEN TO US EITHER.

49

YOU'LL PROBABLY BE REALLY DISAPPOINTED ONCE YOU START INVESTIGATING. HA HA.

I'VE HEARD THEY ARE A SUB-ORGANIZATION OF NEW TRUTH SOCIETY...

OUR GROUP IS NOT EVEN THAT SYSTEMATIC, THOUGH.

WE ARE BASICALLY A STUDY GROUP. THAT'S IT.

BUT... BEING NICE OUT OF FEAR OF BEING RIPPED APART TO DEATH...

CAN YOU REALLY CALL THAT RIGHTEOUSNESS?

IF IT'S NOT FEAR, THEN WHAT MAKES HUMANS REPENT FOR THEIR SINS?

HAVE YOU SEEN ANYTHING LIKE IT?

IF WHAT YOU SAY IS TRUE, THEN THAT GOD YOU'RE SPEAKING OF DOESN'T BELIEVE IN HUMAN AUTONOMY.

AUTONOMY...

YEAH...IT'S IMPORTANT.

WHEN I WAS A KID, I HATED GOING TO CONFESSION.

BAD KIDS DON'T EVEN RECOGNIZE THEIR SINS.

AND ONLY THE GOOD KIDS TRY TO SQUEEZE EVERY LAST DROP OF THEIR SINS FOR CONFESSION.

WHILE IRRESPONSIBLE SINNERS ENJOY COMFORT...

...ONLY THE GOOD ARE BURDENED BY THE WEIGHT OF SIN.

YOU'RE CHAIRMAN JINSOO JUNG, CORRECT?

YES. NICE TO MEET YOU.

PARKING MUST'VE BEEN A NIGHTMARE, RIGHT? IT'S AN OLD NEIGHBORHOOD.

EXCUSE ME FOR A SECOND.

I'M SORRY I COULDN'T SPARE YOU MORE TIME.

FEEL FREE TO CONTACT ME IF YOU NEED ANY HELP.

THEN, I'LL GET GOING.

HE'S DEFINITELY NOT YOUR AVERAGE JOE.

DID YOU EXPECT A CULT LEADER TO SEEM LIKE A NORMAL HUMAN BEING?

KNOCK KNOCK

...

SUNG HO, ARE YOU SLEEPING?

≋SNIFF≋

DON'T WASH IT. I'M GOING TO WEAR IT TOMORROW.

WHAT HAPPENED?

I MET HIM WHILE VOLUNTEERING...

HE WAS TRENDING ON THE INTERNET SO I WENT WITH MY FRIENDS TO SEE WHAT ALL THE FUSS WAS ABOUT.

I'M NOT A FANATIC OR ANYTHING. IT WAS JUST OUT OF CURIOSITY...

I'M NOT GOING TO GO ANYMORE.

THERE'S NOTHING TO WORRY ABOUT, DAD.

Chairman Jinsoo Jung

Q All   🖼 Images   📰 News   ▶ Video   🗺 Maps   ⋮ More

FIREFIGHTING
Brave Citizen Award Presentation

itizen Award Prese

Chairman Jinsoo Jung opens a homeless
shelter with his own money
Faith and Life | 2017. 11. 05 | 📤

Chairman Jinsoo Jung opens a free
convenience store for children in poverty
Future Religion | 2016. 04. 16 | 📤

Sodo Legal Law Office,
Arrowhead Victims' Group
Weekly Issue | 2018. 03. 02 | 📤

Charity and fanaticism, two
faces of New Truth Society
Legal News | 2018. 07. 23 | 📤

Charity and fanaticism, two faces of New Truth Society

apidly becoming known as a place of severe punishment rman Jinsoo Jung's lecture y cannot deny responsibility ing their own doctrines and tures.

h devotee's religious beliefs re shaking the norms of our ety.

Hyejin Min, Lawyer
(Sodo Legal Law Office)

Hyejin Min, Lawyer
(Sodo Legal Law Office)

are prisoners who have serve ntinuously leaking information such as criminal records has tion of lowering the crime rate does not align.

Also, the person who committed the crime and family. Advocates for reducing regulations and for the insanity defense. Opposed to revealing s actions are criticism of rules of law.

he person who c
Advocates for re
insanity defense
s are criticism of

THAT MURDERER WHO KILLED YOUR WIFE...

DO YOU THINK HE'S LIVING IN REPENTANCE?

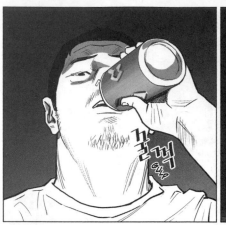

DIVER | Abandoned Building Housewife Murder

Abandoned Building Housewife Murder Victim

Dongsan Daily News | 2015.05.21

A body was found in an abandoned buil[...]
She was a housewife delivering socks a[...]
her husband who was on a stakeout for [...]
Pity...

Abandoned Building Housewife Murder Suspect Arrested

HEY, STOP HIM!

HE'S LOST IT.

MOVE!!

GET OUT OF THE WAY, ASSHOLE!

KYUNG HOON...

KYUNG HOON, PLEASE...

MOVE!

KYUNG HOON JIN! ARE YOU OUT OF YOUR MIND?

DROP THE GUN, YOU BASTARD!

LET ME JUST TAKE A LOOK...

LET ME JUST MAKE SURE...

FUCK! ISN'T THAT OKAY?

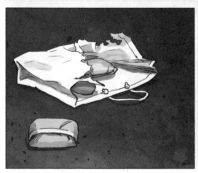

Sujin Jeong
2015.05.19 5:47 Friends only

It's been couple days since Detective Jin came home...
I was going to bring him some socks and underwear but Sung Ho Jin says it's been a while since he last saw dad and that he'll deliver them to him on his way back...
My son is all grown up...Asked him if he's going to be all right going alone and he said he can go with his eyes closed...
Well it's a street that he's been on numerous times to see his dad ever since he was 5 years old. lol

No, but...hahaha
Why'd you bring it back?
If you dropped it somewhere I would've understood...but how can you forget that you had it in your hand all the way back home lol

LMAO I wanted to just laugh in disbelief but I held it in and gave him an earful.
Anyways, Hubby you are going to stink because you can't even change your clothes...that MAN smell.

Welp! going to feed my son dinner and I shall go myself...

 5   25

Hye Eun Shin
LMAO Sung Ho. Nice try.
2015.05.19. 6:20

Hye Eun Shin
Sujin this isn't you right? right?
Pick up the phone Sujin, please...
2015.05.20. 6:20

SUJIN...

WHAT? WHY DID YOU COME IN?!

SUJIN...

SUJIN... HONEY... SUNG HO'S MOTHER...

KYUNG HOON...LET'S LEAVE...

WHO LET HIM IN? GET HIM OUT OF HERE!

Abandoned building murder suspect arrested. Suspect is a male in his forties.

Suspicion of drug use. Proceeding with drug testing.

KYUNG HOON JIN! I TOLD YOU TO TAKE SOME TIME OFF. WHY ARE YOU HERE?

ARE YOU GOING TO PULL OUT YOUR GUN AGAIN?

HOW ARE YOU GOING TO TAKE CARE OF SUNG HO IF YOU'RE LIKE THIS?

YOU HAVE TO STAY STRONG SO SUNG HO HAS SOMEONE TO LEAN ON.

COPS CATCH CRIMINALS.

KYUNG HOON...

WHY DO YOU WANT TO KNOW HOW LONG HIS SENTENCE IS?!

DO YOU THINK YOUR MOM BOUGHT YOU A PHONE TO HAVE YOU SEARCH THINGS LIKE THAT?

I TOLD YOU NOT TO PAY ATTENTION TO THE TRIAL, DIDN'T I?

I TRIED NOT TO...BUT I CAN'T...

I REALLY DON'T WANT TO...BUT I JUST CAN'T.

IT'S TOO SHORT...

HOW COULD THIS HAPPEN...

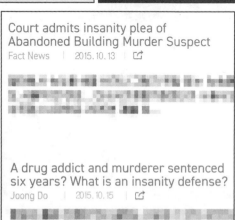

Court admits insanity plea of Abandoned Building Murder Suspect

Fact News | 2015. 10. 13 |

A drug addict and murderer sentenced six years? What is an insanity defense?

Joong Do | 2015. 10. 15 |

Family
Teenager

Comfortable Mind Therapist

I'M GOING TO GO USE THE RESTROOM. I'LL BE RIGHT BACK.

ARE YOU SUNG HO JIN?

...?

YOU'RE SUNG HO, RIGHT?

YEAH...

DID YOU SEE THE TRIAL RESULTS?

WHAT DID YOU THINK?

WHO ARE YOU GUYS?

WHAT ARE YOU GUYS DOING RIGHT NOW?! DO YOU REALLY WANT TO DO THIS TO HIM?

WHAT DO YOU WANT TO HEAR FROM A KID?!

PLEASE JUST LEAVE US ALONE.

LET US LIVE.

I WAS GOING TO TELL THEM...

I WAS JUST ABOUT TO SAY...

WHAT?

I SAID I WAS GOING TO TELL THEM...

I WAS JUST ABOUT TO SAY THAT I'M DEFINITELY GOING TO KILL HIM SOMEDAY...!

WHY WON'T YOU LET ME TALK?!

WHY?

Displaying results

tch ✓ Newest ✓ Oldest

Court admits

Fact News

Abandoned Building drug murderer release nears...
insanity defense controversy rises once again.

Joong Do | 1 day ago |

An ordinary housewife in a familiar residential area was in the middle of
everyday activity...it was an incident that made everyone shudder in fear
suspect tested positive for drugs. Under medical supervision once again

Abandoned Building drug murder suspect
post release management

KBC | 1 day ago |

WHEW.

I'M GOING HOME. SOLD A LOT.

UGH, I SHOULD GET HOME AS WELL.

흥ㄷ다ㄱ
SCURRY

ARE YOU NOT SLEEPING, EUN YOOL?

JEONG...JA...

...PARK...

YOU'RE...
GOING TO
HELL.

FIVE DAYS
FROM NOW, THREE
O'CLOCK *PM*...

FINALLY!! FINALLY!!

HERE IN KOREA! A DEMONSTRATION OF HELL BROKE OUT IN THE MIDDLE OF SEOUL!!

ALL THIS TIME COUNTLESS MESSAGES OF INTENT WERE SENT OUT TO PEOPLE WHO DID NOT CARE TO LOOK OR LISTEN!

AS IF BEING SPOON FED! A DEMONSTRATION FOR A MASSIVE CITY WITH A POPULATION OF TEN MILLION TO SEE! NOT ONLY THAT, IT WAS SHOWN IN BROAD DAYLIGHT!!

BUT EVEN THEN! WHAT ARE WE HUMANS DOING?

WE'RE STILL SAYING THAT IT'S A BLUFF, SPECIAL EFFECTS MAKEUP, AN ACT OF TERROR... SPEWING ALL THAT NONSENSE!

HOW MUCH MORE DO WE HAVE TO SEE FOR US TO FACE REALITY?

MY GOD! AN INVESTIGATION? THEY'RE NUTS! IF A JUDGE DECIDES TO IMPOSE THE DEATH PENALTY, DO YOU INVESTIGATE THE JUDGE?

THIS IS BLASPHEMY! AT THIS POINT IN TIME, WHAT SHOULD THE POLICE BE DOING?

YOUNG HOON JOO! UNCOVER THE TRUTH BEHIND THIS SINNER!

AND LET IT BE KNOWN THAT NO ONE CAN AVOID GOD'S EYE!

WHAT DO YOU THINK GOD'S PURPOSE WAS BY HAVING THE DEMONSTRATION OCCUR RIGHT HERE, RIGHT NOW, IN SEOUL, SOUTH KOREA?

IT'S BECAUSE WE ARE HERE!

ARROWHEAD!! ARROWHEAD!!

IF GOD DREW THE BOW OF DEMONSTRATION, THEN WE...

...HAVE TO FLY!!

79

FLY AND BE EMBEDDED!

WHERE?

INTO PEOPLE LIKE HIM! WRITER KWANGJIN KIM!

LET'S LISTEN TO WHAT HE HAS TO SAY TO US.

HAVING LOW TRUST IN GOVERNMENTAL AUTHORITY CAN'T BE AN EXCUSE FOR PRIVATE SANCTION.

THE ONLY PUNISHMENT FOR IGNORING STATIC PROCEDURE IS LYNCHING.

EVEN IF IT'S GOD'S ORDER, JUST AS THEY SAY, PEOPLE HAVE TO SET THEIR OWN RULES.

RATIONALITY IS THE ONE AND ONLY TOOL THAT HUMAN BEINGS HAVE. IF YOU HAND OVER THE ABILITY TO THINK TO SOMEONE ELSE...

THINK?

JUST DON'T THINK AT ALL!!

A MERE HUMAN BEING! EVEN WHEN GOD IS SHOWING US INTENT WITH HIS OWN HANDS!

WANTS TO THINK? HOW CAN YOU BE SO ARROGANT?

PLEASE DON'T KILL ME... PLEASE SPARE MY LIFE...

WHAT DO YOU WANT? WHY ARE YOU DOING THIS TO ME?

I HAVE A FAMILY. PLEASE...

...PLEASE...

KE KE KE KE.

PLEASE DON'T KILL ME. I HAVE A FAMILYYYY.

IF YOU ARE GOING TO BE THIS FUCKING SCARED, WHY DID YOU TREAT GOD'S INTENT LIKE SHIT?

...

HEY, OLD MAN, WHAT'S YOUR REASON FOR SAYING ALL THAT? HUH?

...WHAT?

DOES IT MAKE YOU SEEM RIGHTEOUS? DO YOU FEEL LIKE AN INTELLECTUAL? DOES IT MAKE YOU FEEL GOOD?

I'M SORRY. I'M SORRY.

WHAT ARE YOU SORRY ABOUT?

...

IF YOU APOLOGIZE, SHOULD WE JUST LET IT GO BY THINKING-- OH, THIS GUY IS SINCERE?

ARE WE A JOKE TO YOU?

I... SELF-RIGHTEOUSLY THOUGHT ONLY MY OPINIONS WERE TRUE WITHOUT RESPECTING YOUR BELIEFS...

CRACK

THUD

THIS FUCKING SINNER IS STILL TRYING TO LECTURE US?

WHEN DID WE EVER ASK YOU FOR YOUR RESPECT?

UGH...

I...I WAS...

...DRUNK OFF OF PEOPLE'S ATTENTION AND MY OWN PRIDE.

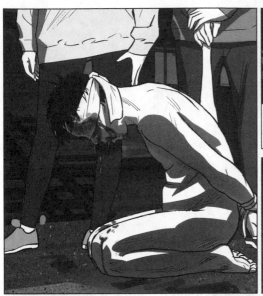

AND TALKED NONSENSE WITHOUT EVEN KNOWING MY PLACE.

I REPENT OF MY ARROGANCE.

FORGIVE ME...

HE DIDN'T EVEN THANK OUR FAMILY MEMBERS WHO LED HIM TO THE RIGHT PATH UNTIL THE VERY END!

BUT WE HAVE MORE IMPORTANT MATTERS AT HAND, RIGHT?

DETECTIVE JIN, YOU REALLY DON'T HAVE THE CRIMINAL RECORD?

I DON'T. EVEN IF I DID, I WOULDN'T TELL YOU.

WHY ARE YOU SO CURIOUS ABOUT A DEAD PERSON'S CRIMINAL RECORD?

IT'S BLOWING UP ON THE INTERNET. WHAT THE CRIME FOR THE JUDGMENT WAS.

PRESS AND MEDIA SHOULD THINK ABOUT SETTING MYTHS STRAIGHT. THIS IS WHY PEOPLE CALL YOU GUYS TRASH REPORTERS.

WHETHER IT'S TRASH REPORTERS OR POLICE DOGS...

...JUST LET ME KNOW IF ANYTHING COMES UP.

WE NEED CRIMINAL FACTS IN ORDER FOR US TO START INVESTIGATING...

WHAT? YOUNG HOON JOO? IF YOU WANT, WE CAN...

HELLO?

WHAT DO YOU MEAN, INVESTIGATE THE VICTIM'S CRIME...?

IF YOU HAVE RECORD OF CRIMINAL CONDUCT, GIVE US THE INFORMATION...

WHAT'S ALL THIS RUCKUS ABOUT?

WHERE ARE THE CALLS FROM? HOW DID THEY KNOW OUR OFFICE NUMBER?

THAT GUY ON THE BROADCAST HAS SOME IMPRESSIVE RESOURCES. HE EVEN KNOWS THE MURDER VICTIM'S IDENTITY...

AND THE WRITER? HOW'S HE DOING?

HE WANTS TO TESTIFY IN PERSON. HE'S HERE WITH HIS LAWYER.

THINK HE'S DOING ALL RIGHT.

HOW ABOUT THE ARROWHEAD GUYS?

CAUGHT A COUPLE ON THE SCENE BUT THEY'RE REFUSING TO MAKE A STATEMENT.

SCENE? THAT WAS A LIVE BROADCAST? THEY GOT SOME GUTS...

HEARD THEY ARE ALL IN THEIR TEENS. I DON'T KNOW IF THEY'RE BEING BRAVE OR STUPID...

I'LL GO SEE THE VICTIM. YOU GO WITH WONPIL AND BEAT SOMETHING OUT OF THEM.

WE'VE GOT TO CATCH THAT GUY WITH THE CHIEF HAT.

YES, SIR.

HELLO.

HUH?

YOU'RE...

HELLO. I'M KWANGJIN KIM'S LAWYER, HYEJIN MIN.

AH...YES. I'M KYUNG HOON JIN.

PLEASE TAKE A SEAT.

DUDE, MOVE.

YOU STINK.

AH...I'M HUNGRY.

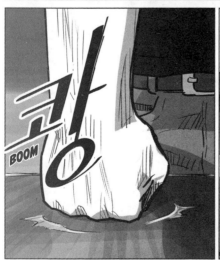

BOOM

EVERYONE, SHUT YOUR MOUTH! OR DO YOU WANT ME TO SHUT IT FOR YOU?

HEY, DETECTIVE JUNG...THEY'RE KIDS.

OOOOOH... TOUGH GUY.

90

LET'S BE NICE AND FINISH THIS UP QUICKLY BEFORE THIS GUY DOES SOMETHING.

SEE? SEE? IT'S JUST LIKE THE MOVIES.

GOOD COP, BAD COP.

SO WHAT? DON'T TALK TO ME.

I WAS HEADING TO THE UNDERGROUND PARKING LOT AFTER MY LECTURE...

...AND THEY SUDDENLY JUMPED ME.

I GOT KNOCKED OUT AFTER A HEAVY BLOW TO THE HEAD. WHEN I WOKE UP, MY HANDS WERE TIED...

DO YOU REMEMBER HOW MANY PEOPLE THERE WERE?

I'M NOT SURE. FROM THE VOICES I HEARD, THERE WERE AROUND SIX PEOPLE...

DID YOU CATCH ALL OF THEM?

WE CAUGHT FOUR OF THEM, BUT...THEY'RE ALL MINORS.

...

IF YOU THINK YOU'LL GET OFF EASY BECAUSE YOU'RE MINORS, YOU'RE WRONG. YOU AREN'T YOUNG OFFENDERS.

ALL OF YOU WILL BE SENT TO JUVIE.

HUH??

WHAT?!

SO IF YOU WANT AN EXTENUATION AT LEAST, DON'T SHIFT BLAME ON EACH OTHER...

...AND ANSWER SINCERELY!

YOU AREN'T YOUNG OFFENDERZZZZ...

BRO, MR. DETECTIVE HERE IS SERIOUS.

OLD MAN, DO YOU THINK PEOPLE WILL STAY QUIET UNTIL OUR TRIAL?

CAN'T YOU TELL THAT IT'S NOT THE WORLD THAT YOU ONCE KNEW, OLD MAN?

AREN'T YOU GUYS THE ONES THAT BELIEVE IN GOING TO HELL IF YOU DO SOMETHING BAD?

KIDNAPPING, ILLEGAL CONFINE- MENT, ASSAULT... THESE ARE ALL SERIOUS CRIMINAL OFFENSES.

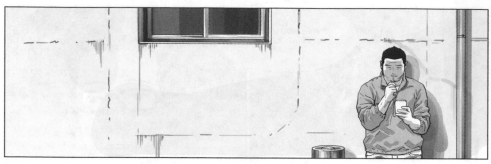

WOW! THEY WON'T EVEN BUDGE!

THEY TRULY BELIEVE THE WORLD IS COMING TO AN END...

NO, NOT THE END...WHAT WAS IT?

THEY SAY IT'S GOING TO BECOME A SANE WORLD.

COMPLETION?

OH.

SO HOW'S SUNG HO? DID YOU SCOLD HIM?

HE SMILED...

...FOR THE FIRST TIME IN SIX YEARS.

REALLY? THAT'S GREAT.

WHAT'S WRONG?

DOESN'T THIS MEAN SUNG HO IS GETTING BETTER?

I HAVE NO IDEA...WHY IS HE LAUGHING?

OR WHY IS HE CRYING?

HEY, WHAT PARENT KNOWS ALL ABOUT THEIR KID?

IF THEY SEEM HAPPY, JUST TAKE IT AS IT IS.

95

YEAH, I'M ALMOST THERE. STAIRS.

I'M WALKING UP THE STAIRS. WHAT'S THE HURRY?

LOCATION: SODO JOINT LAW OFFICE

WHAT? WHO'S...THERE?

MAN...THERE'S EVEN MORE NOW.

KNOW YOUR HUMILIATION? SOME-ONE NEEDS TO TEACH THEM SOME PROPER LANGUAGE.

ATTORNEY MIN, HURRY. TO THE COUNSELING OFFICE.

WHAT'S UP? DID SOMEONE GET TERRORIZED AGAIN?

JUST HEAD IN FIRST.

WHAT...DO YOU THINK THAT IS?

WHATEVER IT IS...

I'LL FIND OUT ON THE DAY OF.

PARDON? CAN YOU REPEAT THAT?

WHAT DID THEY WANT TO DO?

THEY WANT TO BROADCAST MY DEATH.

A LIVE BROADCAST...

CRAZY BASTARDS!!

AND WHAT DID YOU TELL THEM?

THE CHAIRMAN...SAID HE'LL PAY ME ABOUT 2.7 MILLION DOLLARS AS THE BROADCAST FEE.

I DON'T KNOW WHAT THE SAFEST WAY WOULD BE...FOR ME TO RECEIVE SUCH A HUGE SUM OF MONEY.

CAN YOU GUYS HELP ME SO THAT MY KIDS CAN GET THE MONEY?

MISS! YOU SHOULDN'T JUMP TO CONCLUSIONS.

IF IT'S BROADCASTED, NOT ONLY YOURS BUT YOUR CHILDREN'S IDENTITY WILL BE KNOWN TO THE PUBLIC.

BUT WHAT IF IT'S TRUE?

WHAT WILL HAPPEN TO MY CHILDREN IF I DIE IN THE NEXT FEW DAYS?

I CAME TO SEE YOU, ATTORNEY MIN, BECAUSE MY SON DID SOME RESEARCH AND SAID YOU WOULD BE ABLE TO HELP...

IF YOU CAN'T, I'LL FIND SOMEWHERE ELSE.

NO. THANK YOU FOR COMING. WHATEVER NEW TRUTH SOCIETY IS PULLING, I WOULD RATHER HAVE THEM DO IT IN FRONT OF OUR EYES.

ATTORNEY PARK, CAN I HAVE A MINUTE...

WHAT?

CAN I TALK TO YOU FOR A SECOND?

WE'LL BE RIGHT BACK.

ARE YOU REALLY GOING TO LET THEM BROADCAST THIS? THAT'S INSANE.

WHAT'S THE PROBLEM? ARE YOU WORRIED THOSE MONSTERS ARE GOING TO COME OUT?

THEY WON'T. EVEN IF THEY DO, THEY'LL BE CAUGHT.

IF THAT HAPPENS, NEW TRUTH SOCIETY WILL BE HUMILIATED IN FRONT OF THE WHOLE WORLD.

THEY ARE LITERALLY PAYING MONEY TO BE HUMILIATED. WHY WOULD WE STOP THAT?

WHAT IF...THE PROPHECY COMES TRUE?

...

HA HA, ATTORNEY MIN, ARE YOU ACTUALLY BELIEVING THEIR NONSENSE?

YOU SURE CHANGED A LOT AFTER CHASING THEM FOR A COUPLE YEARS.

OKAY, LET'S SAY THE PROPHECY DOES COME TRUE.

WE STILL DON'T HAVE ANY OTHER OPTIONS.

IT'S BETTER TO AT LEAST GET PAID.

THE KIDS WILL BE LEFT BY THEMSELVES...

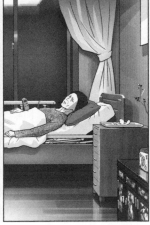

ARE
YOU HERE,
HYEJIN?

MOM, DID YOU NOT EAT ANYTHING, AGAIN?

NO... I HAD HALF AN ORANGE IN THE AFTERNOON...

I JUST THROW UP EVERYTHING I EAT NOW.

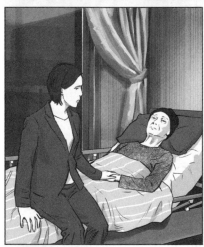

DID SOMETHING HAPPEN? IS THAT WRITER GUY HURT PRETTY BADLY?

WHAT'S HAPPENING ...

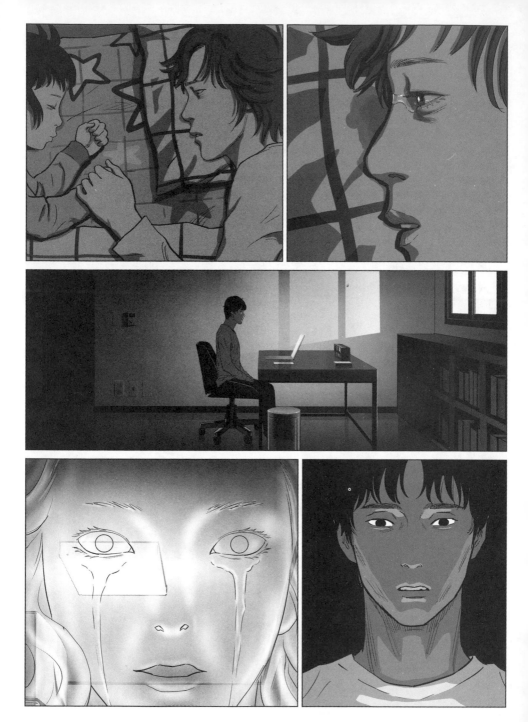

MOM, ARE YOU CRAZY? WHAT KIND OF CANCER PATIENT SMOKES CIGARETTES? I THOUGHT YOU QUIT?

PUT THAT OUT! WE'LL GET COMPLAINTS FROM THE MAINTENANCE OFFICE.

THAT WAS WHEN I HAD A CHANCE OF SURVIVING...

IF THEY CALL, JUST TELL THEM YOU'RE BURNING INCENSE FOR YOUR DEAD MOTHER.

YOU REALLY...

KE KE KE

YOU'RE LAUGHING WHEN YOUR MOTHER IS DYING...

JUST GO FETCH ME AN ASHTRAY.

UM...

WHAT ARE YOU MUMBLING ABOUT?

ISN'T THAT THE ANALYSIS? GIVE IT TO ME!

WHAT? ARROW-HEAD? EVEN IF THEY ARE MINORS, THEY WERE AT THE CRIME SCENE AND IT'S UNCLEAR WHERE THEY LIVE...

BUT HOW'D YOU GET THIS NUMBER?

THIS IS OBSTRUCTION OF JUSTICE...

NO... WHEN DID I THREATEN YOU... HELLO?

HELLO?

HOW DID MY PERSONAL PHONE NUMBER GET LEAKED?

ALL OF YOU, TURN OFF YOUR PHONES.

SO UM...THAT CARCASS ISN'T A PART OF AN ORGANISM...SO BASICALLY, IT'S NOT HUMAN.

THEN WHAT IS IT?

WHAT THE HELL IS THIS? WHAT DO YOU MEAN, IT'S NOT ORGANIC MATTER?

WE'RE STILL NOT SURE WHAT IT IS...

BUT WE'RE SURE IT'S NOT ORGANIC MATTER.

YOU'RE SAYING THAT IT'S FAKE? DO YOU KNOW HOW MANY TIMES WE'VE SEEN DEAD BODIES?

THAT WAS A CORPSE.

HOW DO I REPORT THIS?

DO I SAY THERE'S A MURDER CASE BUT WE ARE UNSURE IF THE THING THAT DIED IS HUMAN OR NOT?

WE REALLY CAN'T FIND ANYTHING WHEN THIS ALL HAPPENED IN BROAD DAYLIGHT WITH HUNDREDS OF EYEWITNESSES?

INCOMING

Attorney Min
010-0000-0000

DIDN'T I TELL YOU TO TURN OFF YOUR PHONE?

TURN IT OFF RIGHT NOW!

HELLO?

YES... YES...

SEEMS LIKE IT'S A REALLY IMPORTANT CALL.

WE MEET AGAIN, CHAIRMAN JINSOO JUNG.

YES, GOOD TO SEE YOU AGAIN, DETECTIVE.

I'M ASSUMING ATTORNEY MIN CONTACTED YOU?

THERE'S A MURDER NOTICE. OF COURSE THE POLICE KNOW.

WHY? WERE YOU PLANNING TO NOT BROADCAST IF THE POLICE GOT INVOLVED?

NO. OF COURSE NOT.

THE MORE THE MERRIER.

I DIDN'T KNOW NEW TRUTH SOCIETY WAS SO LOADED.

WELL...WE HAVE A WIDE VARIETY OF PEOPLE IN OUR GROUP. SOME OF OUR MEMBERS ARE QUITE WEALTHY.

DETECTIVES CHASING AFTER GOD...

SOUNDS SOMEWHAT MYTHICAL.

IT'S MUCH LIKE THE ANCIENTS, FRIGHTENED BY THE ECLIPSE, TRYING TO HUNT THE DOGS THAT SWALLOWED THE SUN.

ISN'T A HUNTER PURSUING A NON-EXISTENT DOG... BETTER?

COPS CATCH. WHETHER IT'S A DOG--

--OR ANYTHING ELSE...

BETTER THAN A CHIEF PRIEST WHO BRINGS HARM TO THE INNOCENT BECAUSE OF HIS BELIEF THAT AN ECLIPSE IS THE WRATH OF GOD.

ATTORNEY HYEJIN MIN?

WE HAVE A LOT TO DO, SO LET'S HEAD IN.

SORRY, I DON'T HAVE MUCH TO OFFER...

OH, NO. DON'T MIND US.

SO... ARE THE KIDS... HOME?

YES, THEY'RE IN THEIR ROOM... WHY?

GOOD. THEY SHOULD REFRAIN FROM GOING OUTSIDE.

THANK YOU FOR THE COFFEE.

WE SHOULD TALK TO THE KIDS.

THEY'RE STILL WITNESSES...

JEONGJA PARK WITNESSED IT TOO. THEY HAVE IT ON THE PHONE AS WELL.

LEAVE THE KIDS ALONE...

BIG BROTHER, WHAT ARE YOU DOING? MOMMY TOLD YOU TO HELP ME WITH COLORING.

WHY AREN'T YOU HELPING? I'M GOING TO TELL ON YOU.

SHHH! QUIET.

HERE... TAKE A LOOK.

I'M GOING TO SAY THIS AGAIN. THE CHILDREN'S IDENTITIES CANNOT BE REVEALED, NO MATTER WHAT.

THAT APPLIES TO JEONGJA PARK'S IDENTITY AS WELL, UNTIL THE BROADCAST STARTS.

DON'T WORRY, NOTHING WILL BE LEAKED FROM OUR SIDE.

EVEN IF THE BROADCAST FALLS THROUGH, WHATEVER THE REASON IS, YOU STILL HAVE TO PAY THE FULL AMOUNT.

SOUNDS LIKE YOU WILL DO EVERYTHING YOU CAN TO STOP THE BROADCAST.

HERE'S THE WRITTEN AGREEMENT.

SORRY, IT WAS A JOKE. I'M NOT USED TO THIS KIND OF SETTING.

AS LONG AS JEONGJA PARK IS HERE AT THE SCHEDULED TIME...

I REALLY DON'T KNOW ABOUT ANY OF THIS, SO PLEASE TAKE CARE OF IT FOR ME.

OF COURSE.

I DON'T CARE WHAT THE OTHER CONDITIONS ARE.

HOW OLD ARE YOUR KIDS?

THIRTEEN AND SIX.

OH, QUITE THE AGE GAP.

MR. CHAIRMAN, I JUST MADE THE ADVANCE PAYMENT OF 1.37 MILLION.

OH.

PLEASE, CHECK.

WE'VE CONFIRMED THE DEPOSIT.

BUT I DON'T SEE A SINGLE PHOTO OF YOUR HUSBAND?

MY KIDS... NEVER HAD A FATHER.

IS THAT EVEN POSSIBLE? WHAT DO YOU MEAN, THEY NEVER HAD A FATHER?

HE SHOULD HAVE BEEN PRESENT AT LEAST UP UNTIL YOU HAD YOUR SECOND CHILD.

I...I'M A SINGLE MOTHER.

BOTH OF MY KIDS HAVE DIFFERENT FATHERS.

MA'AM, YOU DON'T HAVE TO TELL HIM ALL THE DETAILS.

YOU HAVE NO OBLIGATION TO ANSWER THESE KINDS OF QUESTIONS.

I WONDER WHAT THE REASON IS.

NOT ONE...BUT YOU HAD TWO KIDS WITHOUT GETTING MARRIED...

WHAT WERE THEIR FATHERS LIKE?

DID THEY ALREADY HAVE A FAMILY?

WHY WOULD YOU WANT TO KNOW THAT?

BECAUSE...IT'S BETTER TO KNOW WHAT THE REASON IS.

WHY DO YOU WANT TO KNOW?

ISN'T IT OBVIOUS?

WHY?

THE REASON IS WHY JEONGJA PARK IS GOING TO HELL.

ARE YOU ALWAYS LIKE THIS?!

SLAM

SO WHAT IS MY MOM'S SIN?

124

≡SNIFF≡

MOMMY, DON'T CRY...WHY ARE YOU CRYING...

≡SNIFF≡

CHAIRMAN...I DON'T CARE WHAT IT IS...

I DON'T CARE WHAT YOU LABEL MY CRIME AS...

JUST ANYTHING...

ATTORNEY MIN, WAS THE CONTRACT SUCCESSFUL?

WAAAAAAA!

I'M SO FORTUNATE.

I WAS NEVER ABLE TO DO ANYTHING AS A MOTHER. THIS IS MY LUCKY CHANCE.

PLEASE HELP SO THAT MY KIDS CAN LIVE WELL IN A PLACE WHERE NO ONE CAN FIND THEM.

I BEG YOU.

YOU HAVE A MEETING WITH THE LANDLORD. WE SHOULD BE GOOD IF WE HEAD THERE NOW.

WHAT ABOUT THE BROADCASTING STATION?

THEY'RE FIXING THEIR SCHEDULE.

PLEASE HURRY. WE DON'T HAVE MUCH TIME.

DETECTIVE JIN SAID THE SAME THING A WHILE AGO...

DO THE BOTH OF YOU THINK YOU HAVE A PART ON THIS STAGE?

SOMETHING CAN BECOME A VARIABLE...

I'M ACTUALLY ENVIOUS OF YOU TWO FOR YOUR DELUSIONS.

OH...

ATTORNEY, ABOUT THAT ECLIPSE.

THE CHIEF PRIEST GAVE MEANING TO THE PEOPLE.

HAD THE CHIEF PRIEST NOT GIVEN MEANING TO THE ECLIPSE, HUMANITY WOULDN'T BE HERE TODAY.

MANKIND IS A SPECIES THAT SELF-DESTRUCTS WITHOUT MEANING.

WHAT A FREAK, HE REALLY BELIEVES SOMETHING'S GOING TO HAPPEN THE DAY AFTER TOMORROW.

ATTORNEY MIN, WHAT ARE YOU SO WORRIED ABOUT?

NO ONE WILL BELIEVE THAT CULT LEADER. THERE WON'T BE A SINGLE STATION THAT WILL LIVE BROADCAST A CRIME SCENE.

PROBABLY ONLY A FEW OF THOSE ARROWHEAD GUYS WILL WATCH IT ON STREAM.

THE KIDS...WHAT ARE YOU GOING TO DO ABOUT THEM?

THE ARROWHEAD GUYS ARE DEFINITELY GOING TO LOOK FOR THEM ONCE THE BROADCAST GOES ON AIR.

I'LL BE SENDING THEM TO A COLLEAGUE IN CANADA FOR NOW.

IF NOTHING HAPPENS, I'LL HAVE THEM COME BACK OR HAVE JEONGJA PARK MOVE TO CANADA...

EVEN THE ARROWHEAD GUYS WILL BE LET DOWN ONCE THEY SEE ALL THE GIMMICKS TWO DAYS FROM NOW.

IMMIGRATION, MY ASS...THEY ARE GOING TO LIVE IN LUXURY WITH THE 2.7 MILLION DOLLARS HERE IN KOREA.

WHAT JEONGJA PARK SAID IS TRUE, ISN'T IT?

JUST PLAY ALONG WITH THOSE MANIACS A LITTLE AND YOU MAKE 2.7 MILLION. THAT'S GOOD LUCK.

YOU GOT TO MAKE IT INTO GOOD LUCK.

IT'LL BE OVER IN TWO DAYS. NO DOUBT.

BOOOIIING!

SURPRISE! BIG SURPRISE!

AN AMAZING ANNOUNCEMENT FROM NEW TRUTH SOCIETY!! NEW TRUTH SOCIETY IS FINALLY PUTTING IN SOME WORK!

New Truth Society
5 hours ago

WE HAVE SOMEONE WHO RECEIVED THE NOTICE FROM HELL IN OUR COUNTRY!!

Very important here at New Tr[u]
Couple of days ago in Seoul, South
New Truth Society told us about the news.
After analyzing the video of the notice that the person directly involved filmed, we have confirmed that the video is not fake.
A notice given right after the demonstration that happened only a few days ago on the streets of Seoul

New Truth Society ✔

@NewTruth

THAT'S NOT ALL!! WHAT'S EVEN MORE SHOCKING IS THAT--

--THEY ARE GOING TO LIVE BROADCAST THE SINNER GOING TO HELL!!

ARROWHEAD! ARROWHEAD!

HOW HAS MY FAMILY BEEN?

HOW MUCH DID YOU HAVE TO SUFFER AMONG THE BLIND?

BUT!! IN TWO DAYS, EVERY CITIZEN, EVERY HUMAN BEING ON EARTH, WILL HEAR US!!

ALL OF YOUR HARDSHIPS WERE A PART OF THE PREPARATION FOR THIS VERY MOMENT!

BUT NEW TRUTH SOCIETY, WHY WON'T YOU REVEAL THE SINNER'S IDENTITY AND WHAT THE CRIME IS?

the video of
right after th

Devotee 204 This is a very in
Our influence to New Truth S
We don't want to miss this a

Devo

THE NEW WORLD IS ALREADY HERE! WHY CAN'T YOU JUST LET GO OF THE OLD WORLD'S WAYS?!

Devotee 582 Even the Chairm
doesn't have any idea. Have to
if no people will receive judgm
not knowing

Devotee 38 You guys already st

Devotee 38 You guys already started

Devotee 1821 He's here!!!

Devotee 204 Sir 38 has arrived

Devotee 177 Everyone keep your ha
off the keyboard

Devotee 38 Notice subject

Devotee 38 Jeongja Park (38 yo. F)

Devotee 38 son Eun Yool Park (13) daughter Ha Yool Park (6)
Single mother, Children have different fathers

135

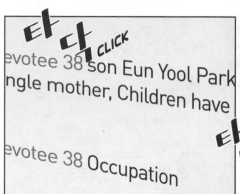

evotee 38 son Eun Yool Park
ngle mother, Children have

evotee 38 Occupation

WOOOW!
THAT'S OUR
DEVOTEE 38!!

ARROWHEAD!
ARROWHEAD!

Trending News

1 Jeongja Park

2 New Truth Society

3 Jeongja Park Notice Vid

4 Jeongja Park's Son Sch

FUCKING...

HEY, SUNG HO.

LOOKS LIKE DAD'S GOT TO HEAD OUT AGAIN...

SUNG HO.

138

YEAH, DAD.

WHERE ARE YOU AT THIS HOUR?

I'M AT MY FRIEND'S HOUSE. I WAS JUST ABOUT TO CALL YOU.

WE'RE PULLING AN ALL-NIGHTER FOR MIDTERMS AND GOING TO GO STRAIGHT TO SCHOOL.

YOU'RE OKAY WITH THAT, RIGHT?

OH, UM...

WHICH FRIEND?

YOU DON'T KNOW HIM. WHY? I CAN'T?

OH, NO...

DON'T STAY UP ALL NIGHT. TRY TO GET SOME SLEEP IN. OKAY?

DAD.

YEAH?

I DON'T HAVE THAT MUCH WILLPOWER.

I WON'T LAST ALL NIGHT, ANYWAY.

RIGHT...

OKAY.

OH, DAD. I GOT TO GO.

IT'S ALL RIGHT. PLEASE REMAIN SEATED.

WAS THAT YOUR DAD? I SAW HIM TODAY, ACTUALLY...

SUNG HO.

THANK YOU FOR DECIDING TO DO THIS.

YES...

FROM NOW ON...

...I'M GOING TO PROCEED ONLY WITH THE TWO OF US INVOLVED.

I'M TELLING YOU THIS AGAIN, BUT THIS ISN'T REVENGE FOR YOUR MOTHER.

IF THERE IS EVEN A SLIGHT VENGEANCE OR HATRED MIXED INTO YOUR DECISION, PLEASE GO BACK NOW.

NO.

MY DECISION IS SOLELY FOR THE *INTENT* TO BE KNOWN.

YES, ATTORNEY MIN. THIS IS KYUNG HOON JIN.

DID YOU SEE ON THE INTERNET?

YEAH, I DID.

I SHOULDN'T HAVE BELIEVED THE NEW TRUTH SOCIETY GUYS!

I'M ON MY WAY TO JEONGJA PARK'S HOUSE RIGHT NOW.

I'D BETTER GET THE KIDS TO SAFETY RIGHT AWAY.

RIGHT NOW? THEN I'LL HEAD--

NO. WE DON'T HAVE TIME. I'LL SEE YOU AT THE AIRPORT.

YES, KYUNG HOON!

HEY, EUN PYO. JEONGJA PARK'S IDENTITY HAS BEEN LEAKED!

TAKE SOME BACKUP WITH YOU AND ARREST ANYONE WHO TRIES TO APPROACH HER!

WHAT ABOUT YOU?

I'M HEADING TO THE AIRPORT.

AIRPORT?

WE'RE FLYING THE KIDS OUT.

WOW! MS. JEONGJA PARK!

DEMONSTRATION SUBJECT'S NAME IS JEONG! JA! PARK!

WHAT DID SHE DO TO BE SENT TO HELL?

SHE HAS TWO KIDS FROM TWO DIFFERENT PEOPLE, BUT NOT A SINGLE FATHER?

145

OUR FAMILY MEMBERS HAVE TO QUICKLY ISOLATE AND PROTECT THESE CHILDREN!

뿌아아앙 VROOM

THERE IS A HIGH CHANCE THAT THESE KIDS ARE VICTIMS OF ABUSE.

AND THEY MIGHT BE THE ONLY ONES WHO CAN TESTIFY TO JEONGJA PARK'S CRIMES!

OUR FAMILY MEMBERS! PLEASE HURRY!

HURRY UP! HURRY UP!

202

확 SWOOSH

DON'T
LOOK AT
YOUR PHONE!

SIGN: LAST STOP SUPERMARKET

CRACK

GULP GULP

THE CRIMINAL BEHIND YOUR MOTHER'S MURDER.

THAT'S WHAT...

...HE LOOKS LIKE.

IS THIS YOUR FIRST TIME SEEING HIM?

THEY'VE NEVER SHOWN HIS FACE. NOT ON *TV* OR IN THE NEWSPAPER.

IT MUST'VE BEEN PAINFUL FOR A LONG TIME TO HATE SOMEONE WHOSE NAME AND FACE YOU DON'T KNOW.

ARE YOU STILL IN PAIN?

...

NO. I'M OKAY NOW.

GOOD...

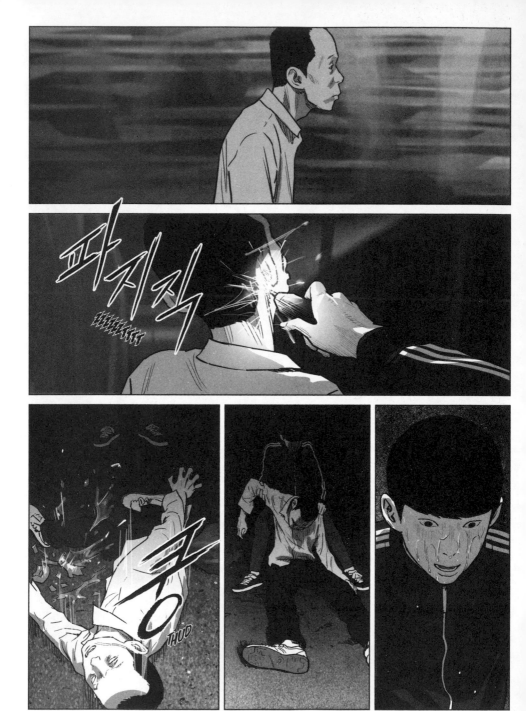

YOU HAVE TO HURRY TO THE DEPARTURE GATE.

HURRY UP AND TAKE CARE OF YOUR SISTER, EUN YOOL...

HUH? WE'RE AT THE AIRPORT. ARE WE GOING ON A TRIP?

I THOUGHT WE WERE GOING WHEN BIG BROTHER IS ON VACATION.

EUN YOOL... YOU ARE GOING NOW...

TOK

TOK

WHEN YOU ARRIVE, SOMEONE FROM OUR COMPANY IS GOING TO BE THERE.

THIS GENTLEMAN IS GOING TO TAKE CARE OF YOU UNTIL YOU GET ON THE PLANE.

I'LL BRING YOUR MOM WITH ME WHEN EVERYTHING IS OVER.

DON'T LOOK AROUND AND TAKE GOOD CARE OF YOUR SISTER. GOT IT?

EUN YOOL.

EUN YOOL.

EUN YOOL! MY LEGS HURT!

HUH?

OH, OKAY...

ARE YOU OKAY? DO YOU WANT ME TO HOLD HER?

NO, I'M FINE.

HA...

WHEN IS MOM COMING?!

I ASKED YOU AGAIN AND AGAIN! WHY ARE YOU ACTING LIKE YOU CAN'T HEAR ME?

MO... MOM...

MOM...

165

DID THE KIDS GET ON THE PLANE?

YES. THEY'RE ON BOARD, SAFELY.

LOOK.

Thank you for using our airline's Unaccompanied Minor Program. We will take them safely and comfortably to their destination.

AH...

AH...

AAAAHHH!!!!!

I COULDN'T EVEN GIVE THEM A HUG...

MY BABIES... I COULDN'T EVEN HUG THEM...

IT'S ALL RIGHT.

YOU'RE GOING TO SEE THEM SOON.

YOU'LL SEE THEM.

167

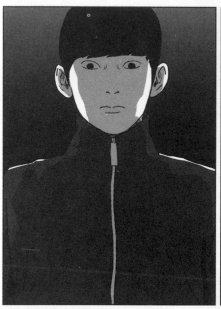

YOU SHOW THEM THE EVIDENCE.

SHOW IT TO THEM AGAIN.

AND AGAIN... NO MATTER HOW MANY TIMES THEY SEE IT, PEOPLE DON'T CHANGE.

"IT'S YOUR FAULT."

REGISTRATION

IT'S NOT THEIR PROBLEM UNTIL THEY THEMSELVES RECEIVE THE NOTICE.

"WHY PUNISH US WHEN YOU CREATED US TO BE SINFUL BEINGS?

LIKE A CHILD WHO RESENTS THEIR PARENTS FOR GIVING BIRTH TO THEM AS A FAILURE...

TOO LAZY TO PUT IN THE EFFORT TO BECOME A GOOD CHILD.

RIP RIP

EXCUSES AFTER EXCUSES...

SHEEEK

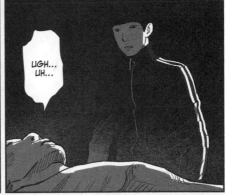

UGH... UH...

HUH?

YOU SHOULDN'T BE UP RIGHT NOW.

UGH...

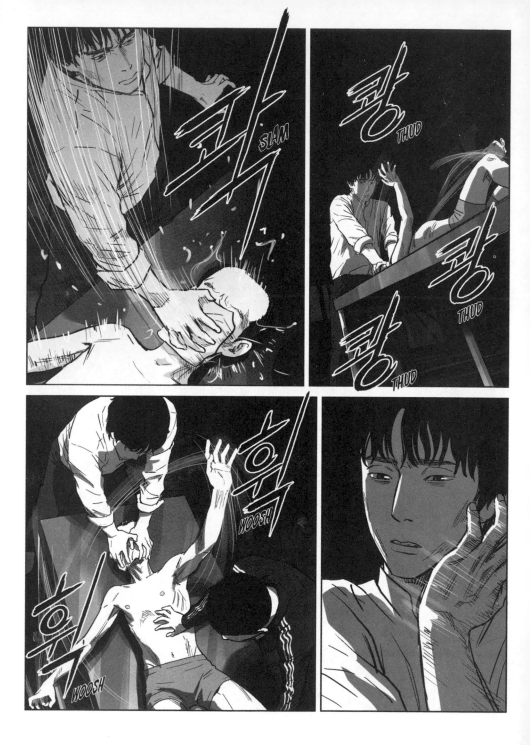

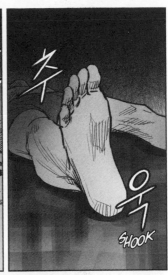

SHOOK

YOU CAN'T BE SLEEPING TOO DEEPLY.

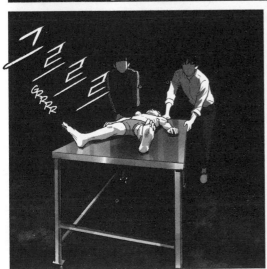

GRRRR

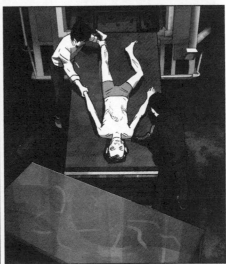

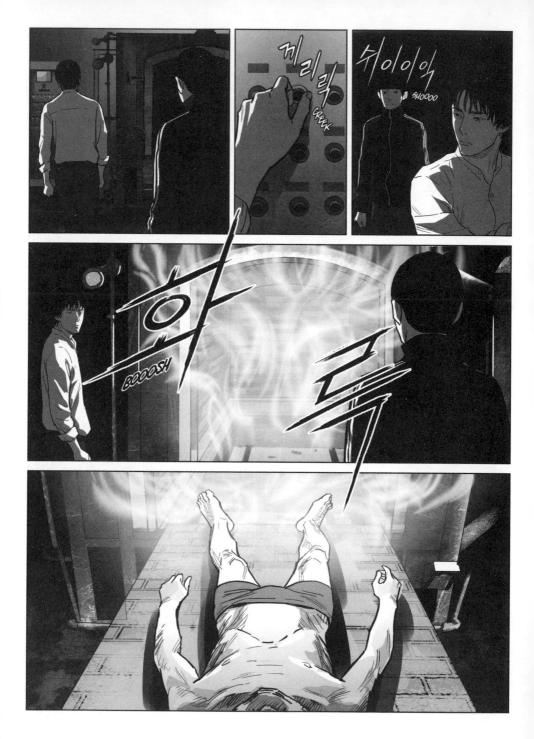

AGGGH!

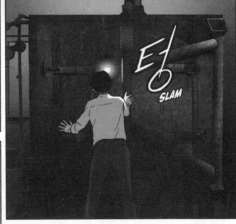

ㅌㅇ
SLAM

AAAAHHHH!

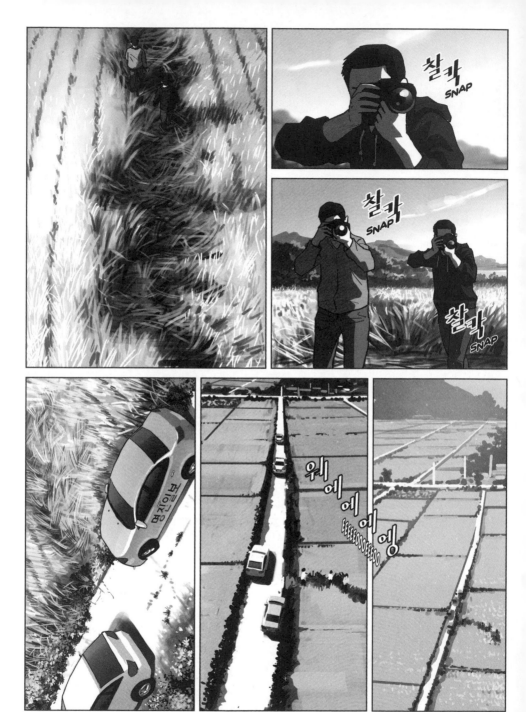

CAR: MYUNG-JIN DAILY NEWS

THE NUMBER YOU HAVE DIALED ...IS NOT AVAILABLE.

HUH?

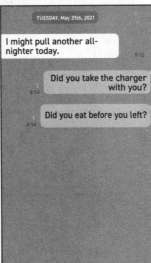

TUESDAY, May 25th, 2021

I might pull another all-nighter today.
8:32

Did you take the charger with you?
8:54

Did you eat before you left?
8:54

177

...?

DID YOU JUST GET HERE?

YEAH...DID SOMETHING HAPPEN?

DID YOU NOT...SEE THE NEWS?

NEWS? WHAT NEWS?

YOU SHOULD GO SEE THE CHIEF, FIRST.

KNOCK KNOCK

COME IN.

I'M CURRENTLY AT JIN YANG CITY, WHERE THE BODY WAS DISCOVERED...

DID YOU CALL ME?

YEAH. COME TAKE A LOOK AT THIS.

AN ANONYMOUS INFORMANT FOUND A STRANGE AREA IN THE RICE FIELD THAT WAS TRAMPLED BY SOMETHING...

THE BODY SEEMS TO BEAR MUCH RESEMBLANCE TO THE ONE THAT WAS FOUND IN THE MONSTER MURDER CASE IN SEOUL. ON TOP OF THAT, THE VICTIM'S IDENTITY HAS BEEN REVEALED.

GOD IS NOT A SUBJECT OF INVESTIGATION

OBEY

ACCORDING TO THE POLICE, THEY ARE HAVING TROUBLE INVESTIGATING THE CASE DUE TO THE HIGH NUMBER OF PROTESTERS AT THE SCENE...

TORN CLOTHES AND AN I.D. WERE FOUND NEAR THE BODY, WHICH SEEM TO HAVE BELONGED TO THE VICTIM.

IT APPEARS THE I.D. BELONGED TO THE CULPRIT BEHIND THE ABANDONED BUILDING HOUSEWIFE MURDER CASE THAT OCCURRED SIX YEARS AGO.

THE MURDERER WAS RECENTLY RELEASED FROM PRISON AND LIVED HERE IN JIN YANG CITY AFTER SIX YEARS IN CUSTODY, DURING WHICH HE RECEIVED TREATMENT AFTER HIS INSANITY PLEA.

...

YOU HAVE TO CALL THE COPS IF YOU FIND A BODY...

WHY DID THE PERSON CALL A REPORTER...? CAN YOU EVEN PRESERVE THE SITE?

THAT...IS THAT... ARE YOU SURE IT'S REALLY HIM?

WE ARE SURE, GIVEN THE CURRENT CIRCUMSTANCES...

...BUT WOULD DOING A *DNA* TEST WITH THAT BODY EVEN HELP?

THERE'S NOTHING TO WORRY ABOUT WITH YOU, RIGHT?

WHAT?

I'M ASKING IF YOU HAVE A SOLID ALIBI.

LAST NIGHT, JEONGJA PARK'S ATTORNEY TOLD ME SHE WAS GOING TO FLY THE KIDS OUT, SO I FOLLOWED HER THERE.

SPENT ALL NIGHT AROUND JEONGJA PARK'S HOUSE FOR A STAKEOUT.

OKAY...DON'T WORRY ABOUT THAT CASE...

BECAUSE OF THIS INCIDENT, THERE'S GOING TO BE A LOT OF INTEREST IN TOMORROW'S BROADCAST.

WE HAVE TO CATCH THEM TOMORROW.

IF WE CATCH THEM, ALL THIS SHIT WILL BE OVER.

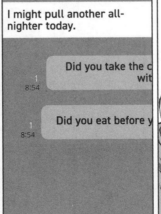

I might pull another all-nighter today.

Did you take the c with

8:54

Did you eat before y

8:54

SIX YEARS AGO, A WOMAN WAS BRUTALLY MURDERED ON HER WAY TO DELIVER...

...SOME UNDERWEAR AND SOCKS TO HER UNDERCOVER COP HUSBAND.

THE SUSPECT DID NOT RECEIVE ANY SORT OF PUNISHMENT AT ALL.

HE WAS ADMITTED TO A HOSPITAL AND RECEIVED TREATMENT!

BECAUSE HE WAS A DRUG ADDICT!

BECAUSE HE DIDN'T INTEND TO COMMIT THE CRIME!

MANKIND DID NOT PUNISH HIM!

BUT GOD DID!

AFTER PATIENTLY WATCHING HIS PEOPLE--THOSE THAT COULDN'T EVEN FOLLOW A SIMPLE RULE OF PUNISHMENT--FOR THOUSANDS OF YEARS...

...GOD SAID, ENOUGH IS ENOUGH, AND HE IS NOW TAKING MATTERS INTO HIS OWN HANDS!

HE IS DELIVERING US A MESSAGE PRIOR TO TOMORROW'S DEMONSTRATION!

JEONGJA PARK!! PLEASE CONFESS YOUR SINS!!

DO THE MOST MEANINGFUL THING YOU CAN DO FOR YOUR LAST DAY!!

THOSE OF YOU THAT KNOW JEONGJA PARK, YOU HAVE A DUTY TO MAKE HER CONFESS HER SINS!

CONFESS YOUR SIN!

REPENT!!!

REPENT!

REPENT!

ATONE FOR YOUR SIN!

ATONE FOR YOUR SIN!

ATONE FOR YOUR SIN!

ATONE FOR YOUR SIN!

LET'S TAKE ALL HER STUFF OUT AND PUT IT BACK IN PLACE AFTER...

GOT IT.

CAN'T YOU GUYS COME BACK LATER?

I'M SORRY, WE'RE REALLY SHORT ON TIME.

DID YOU WANT TO GO SOME-WHERE ELSE INSTEAD?

HOW ARE YOU GOING TO STAY HERE UNTIL TOMORROW?

ARE YOU SURE YOU CAN COME BACK?

REPENT!! REPENT!!!

IF YOU DON'T MAKE IT ON TIME, IT'S A BREACH OF CONTRACT.

NO...I'M STAYING HERE.

IT'S BETTER HERE.

WOOOOOOOO!

WOOOOOO!

ATTORNEY PARK, WHAT IS IT? WHAT'S GOING ON?

THEY'RE NUTS...

EVERY ONE OF THEM IS INSANE...

WHY? WHAT'S HAPPENING?

THE BROADCAST...

EVERY STATION IS GOING TO DO A LIVE BROADCAST TOMORROW...

EVEN ALL OF THE INTERNATIONAL CHANNELS...

185

ARE YOU SURE THE MURDER VICTIM WAS THAT SUSPECT?

YEAH...WE'RE PRETTY POSITIVE...

ARE THERE ANY WITNESSES OR SURVEILLANCE FOOTAGE?

WE CAN'T EVEN INVESTIGATE THE SITE PROPERLY BECAUSE THERE ARE TOO MANY PEOPLE.

THEY'RE GETTING IN THE POLICE'S WAY, SO WE CAN'T EVEN GATHER EVIDENCE...

THERE IS SURVEILLANCE FOOTAGE NEAR THE ALLEYWAY OF THE PERPETRATOR'S HOUSE...

IT'S TOO DARK TO MAKE ANYTHING OUT OF IT.

I'M SORRY, BUT I WOULD LIKE TO TAKE A LOOK AT THE FOOTAGE.

SURE. I'LL SEND OVER THE FILE ONCE I GET BACK TO THE STATION.

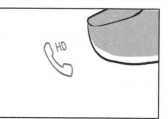

189

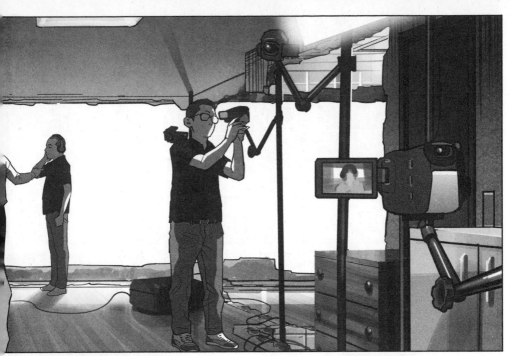

THE *VIP'S* ARE ENTERING.

HOW MUCH DO YOU THINK THOSE PEOPLE SPENT TO WATCH THIS?

SO THAT'S WHERE THE 2.7 MILLION CAME FROM...

NEW TRUTH SOCIETY SEEMS TO BE BIGGER THAN WE EXPECTED.

HOW CAN ALL THIS BE MADE POSSIBLE IN ONLY THREE DAYS?

OH, RIGHT.

SOMEONE FROM THE OFFICE TOLD ME THIS WAS FOR YOU, ATTORNEY MIN.

TO:
Attorney
Hyejin Min

HUH? WHEN DID YOU GET HERE, KYUNG HOON?

SHOULDN'T YOU BE RESTING?

I DON'T SEE CHAIRMAN JINSOO JUNG.

HAVE YOU SEEN HIM?

HE'S PROBABLY WAITING TO APPEAR AT THE PERFECT MOMENT.

HE'S DEFINITELY WATCHING FROM SOMEWHERE.

ARE THE SNIPERS IN PLACE?

YES.

DOUBLE-CHECK.

SIR, ARE YOU CLEAR ON STANDBY?

WE'RE CLEAR ON STANDBY.

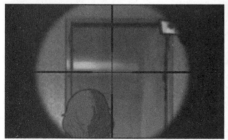

IT'S TIME.

199

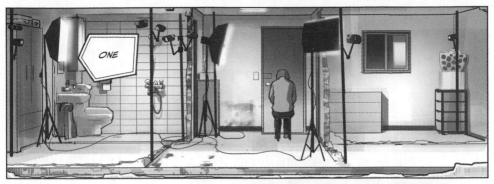

BAM

205

HURRY!

FIRE!! I SAID FIRE!!

START SHOOTING!

FIRE!

SHOOT!

I SAID SHOOT!

SNIPER TEAM!!

206

FIRE!!! I'M TELLING YOU TO START SHOOTING!

AHH...

AHHH...

CRACK

AGGGHH!

DAMN IT!

AAAAAAKK!

PLEASE...

PLEASE...

AAH...DEAR LORD...

BANG

BANG

BANG

SIGN: REAL ESTATE

212

AH...

FLOP

A...
ATTORNEY
MIN...

...

SOMETHING
TERRIBLE HAS
HAPPENED.

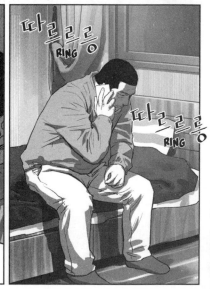

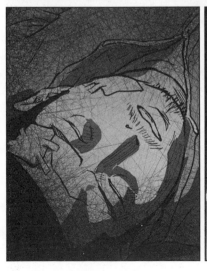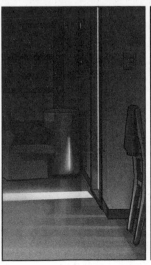

SOMETHING SO SHOCKING HAS HAPPENED THAT WORDS CANNOT DESCRIBE THIS PHENOMENON.

I'M SURE MOST VIEWERS HAVE ALREADY SEEN AND HEARD ABOUT YESTERDAY'S EVENTS THROUGH MULTIPLE MEDIA OUTLETS.

I BELIEVE EVERYONE HAS THEIR EYES ON THIS MAN.

JUST IN A DAY, HE HAS BECOME THE MOST IMPORTANT FIGURE IN KOREA.

TURNS OUT, WE'VE REPORTED ON THIS GENTLEMAN ON SEVERAL OCCASIONS.

I'M SURE EVERYONE REMEMBERS THIS INCIDENT.

A BRAVE YOUNG MAN WHO WITNESSED A DRUNK CITIZEN FALLING ONTO THE SUBWAY TRACKS...

...RESCUED HIM BY JUMPING DOWN WITHOUT HESITATION WHILE THE TRAIN WAS COMING IN.

IT WAS THIS GENTLEMAN.

THERE WAS ANOTHER INCIDENT.

A MAN WHO JUST HAPPENED TO BE PASSING BY THE SCENE OF A FIRE...

...JUMPED INTO DANGER...

...AND SAVED A FOUR-YEAR-OLD CHILD AND HIS MOTHER. I'M SURE YOU ALL REMEMBER.

IT WAS THIS MAN.

THERE WAS YET ANOTHER INCIDENT THAT SURPRISED EVERYONE.

AN UNARMED CITIZEN APPROACHED A MAN SWINGING A KNIFE ON THE SIDEWALK AND PERSUADED HIM TO DROP HIS WEAPON.

WOULD YOU BELIEVE ME IF I SAID THIS WAS ALL DONE BY THE SAME PERSON?

THIS MAN WAS ALSO THE SAME PERSON THAT CONTINUOUSLY WARNED US OF THE RECENT PHENOMENON...

What is intention?

...OVER THE PAST TEN YEARS.

IT'S A SHAME THAT NONE OF US LISTENED TO HIM.

WE NOW BEGIN OUR INTERVIEW WITH NEW TRUTH SOCIETY'S CHAIRMAN, JINSOO JUNG.

THIS INTERVIEW WILL BE BROADCAST NATIONWIDE AND ON THE INTERNET.

HELLO, CHAIRMAN.

YES, HELLO.

NICE TO MEET YOU.

MANY OF US ARE IN SHOCK AND HAVE PUT OUR DAILY LIVES ON HOLD DUE TO YESTERDAY'S CHAOS.

I BELIEVE WE ARE IN DESPERATE NEED OF YOUR ADVICE, CHAIRMAN.

YES, I'M SURE EVERYONE NEEDED SOME TIME TO THINK ABOUT GOD'S MESSAGE.

ISN'T IT A VERY NATURAL REACTION?

HOWEVER, BEING IDLE FOR FEAR OF DOING EVIL SHOULDN'T BE THE SOLUTION.

YOU NEED TO CARRY ON WITH YOUR DAILY LIVES AND ACTIVELY PURSUE GOOD DEEDS.

224

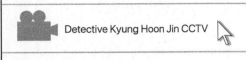
Detective Kyung Hoon Jin CCTV

딸깍
CLICK

Name	Size	

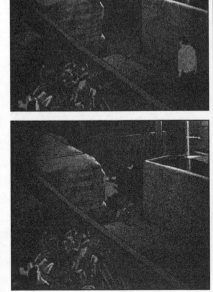

OUT OF THE THREE DEMONSTRATIONS THAT HAPPENED RECENTLY, EXCLUDING THE DRUG ADDICT MURDER INCIDENT...

...YOUNG HOON JOO FROM THE HAPSEONG STATION AND YESTERDAY'S SUBJECT, JEONGJA PARK.

WHAT WERE THEIR CRIMES?

AS FOR THEIR SINS, NEW TRUTH SOCIETY IS DOING ITS BEST TO TRACK DOWN THEIR SINS EVEN AS WE SPEAK, BUT...

...THERE'S A LIMIT TO HOW MUCH INFORMATION WE CAN GATHER AS A PRIVATE ORGANIZATION.

IN JEONGJA PARK'S CASE, IMPORTANT WITNESSES HAVE ALREADY FLED TO A DIFFERENT COUNTRY.

AND I BELIEVE CERTAIN POLICEMEN AND LAWYERS WERE INVOLVED WITH THEIR ESCAPE.

I ASK NOT ONLY FOR THE ORDINARY CITIZENS THAT ARE WATCHING THIS BROADCAST...

...BUT GOVERNMENT AGENCIES, INCLUDING PROSECUTORS AND THE POLICE, TO BREAK AWAY FROM THEIR HABITS.

AND TAKE INITIATIVE.

I'M SURE EVERYONE WATCHING THIS BROADCAST WILL HAVE SIMILAR QUESTIONS.

WHY ARE THESE PHENOMENA HAPPENING MORE FREQUENTLY THESE DAYS?

GOD'S INTERVENTION IN HUMAN AFFAIRS HAS EXISTED ALL THROUGHOUT THE HISTORY OF MANKIND.

UNLESS ALL THE TESTIMONIES FROM VARIOUS RELIGIOUS GROUPS WERE LIES.

THEREFORE, WE SHOULD BE ASKING, "WHY HAVEN'T WE SEEN IT ALL THIS TIME?" NOT "WHY NOW?"

AROUND THE TWENTIETH CENTURY, RATIONALITY BECAME A PREDOMINANT VALUE IN SOCIETY.

WHATEVER WAS OUTSIDE THE NARROW BOUNDARIES OF THAT RATIONALITY WAS DENIED RECOGNITION.

THE FACT THAT I'VE BEEN SAYING THE SAME THING FOR THE PAST TEN YEARS BUT ONLY NOW AM ABLE TO TALK TO YOU LIKE THIS...IS THE PROOF.

PERHAPS THAT IS WHY GOD IS BEING MORE SPECIFIC AND ARTICULATE ABOUT REVEALING HIS INTENTIONS.

SO HE CAN DELIVER HIS MESSAGE CLEARLY.

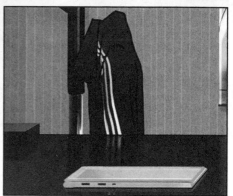

HE'S ASKING US, "IS THIS ENOUGH FOR YOU TO UNDERSTAND?"

THAT...MESSAGE... ACCORDING TO NEW TRUTH SOCIETY, IS THAT HUMAN BEINGS HAVE TO BE EVER SO RIGHTEOUS...

IT'S SOMETHING THAT'S TOO OBVIOUS BUT ABSTRACT AT THE SAME TIME...

THE FACT THAT MANKIND HAS NEVER BEEN ABLE TO ACHIEVE THAT OBVIOUS THING THROUGHOUT EXISTENCE...

...IS GOD'S COMPLAINT!

BASED ON 132 NOTICES AND DEMONSTRATIONS INVESTIGATED BY NEW TRUTH SOCIETY...

...WE PUT TOGETHER A COLLECTION OF CASES ON OUR WEBSITE THAT ANALYZE THE SUBJECTS' CRIMES.

IT'S A DOCUMENT CALLED *"INTENT."*

ONCE YOU SEE THE DOCUMENT YOU'LL GET A CLEARER IDEA ON WHAT GOD WANTS FROM US AND WHAT HE IS FORBIDDING.

SOON, *"INTENT"* WILL BE DISTRIBUTED IN VARIOUS FORMS SO THAT THE WHOLE NATION CAN HAVE EASY ACCESS TO IT.

CORRECT, I ALSO STAYED UP ALL NIGHT READING THE DOCUMENT.

MAYBE IT'LL BECOME A BIBLE FOR THE NEW ERA, WHO KNOWS.

BUT IN A COMPLEX WORLD LIKE TODAY'S SOCIETY, I BELIEVE IT WILL BE DIFFICULT TO DEFINE WHAT JUSTICE IS IN OUR DAILY LIVES WITH ONLY THE CASES GIVEN IN THE *"INTENT."*

NOT EVERYONE CAN LIVE LIKE YOU, CHAIRMAN...

NO! EVERY MOMENT, WE CAN SENSE WHAT IS RIGHT.

GOD GAVE US THAT ABILITY.

IT'S JUST THAT WHEN YOU ARE GIVEN A CHOICE BETWEEN GOOD AND EVIL, IT'S DIFFICULT TO BEAT EVIL'S TEMPTATION.

CHOICE IS JUST A FANCY NAME FOR PUNISHMENT.

THANK YOU... I WISH TO HEAR MORE FROM YOU BUT UNFORTUNATELY, WE ARE OUT OF TIME.

I HOPE TO SEE YOU MORE OFTEN.

I'M SORRY, BUT I CAN'T PROMISE THAT.

I'VE SERVED MY PURPOSE BY TELLING YOU ALL ABOUT THE "INTENT."

I PLAN ON PURSUING GOD ALONE UNTIL I HAVE ANOTHER CALLING.

WELCOME... TO THE NEW WORLD.

DON'T LET YOUR GUARD DOWN, MY DEAR FAMILY MEMBERS! IF WE GET TOO EXCITED, WE'LL BE DOOMED!

DO YOU THINK THE WORLD IS GOING TO CHANGE ITSELF JUST BECAUSE EVERYONE WATCHED YESTERDAY'S BROADCAST?

NO WAY! MAN'S STUPIDITY IS INCREDIBLY... INCREDIBLY...

...INCREDIBLY RESILIENT!!

THEY MIGHT SHOW SIGNS OF REPENTANCE FOR NOW, BUT...

...WHEN THE DEMONSTRATIONS BECOME SPARSE AND PEOPLE LIKE SCHOLARS, WRITERS, AND LAWYERS START TALKING OUT OF THEIR ASSES AGAIN...

...THE WORLD WILL REVERT BACK IN A FLASH!

LOOK AT THEM!

WHEN EVERYONE WAS BOWING BEFORE GOD, THESE TWO WERE JUST STANDING UP STRAIGHT. THEY LOOK FAMILIAR, RIGHT?

"Human rights don't choose people."

Inmate and ex-convict human r[...]
Hyejin Min, Lawyer (bottom lef[...]

IT'S THEM. THE ONES THAT HAVE BEEN A HINDRANCE IN EVERYTHING WE DO.

SIMON'S LIPS ARE BLUE.

PLAY A LITTLE MORE AND HEAD BACK IN.

JUNG HWA ORPHANAGE

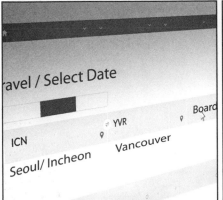

ravel / Select Date

YVR

Board

ICN

Vancouver

Seoul/ Incheon

달칵
CLICK

달칵
CLICK

MOM, WHAT ARE YOU DOING?

MOM...JUST WEAR YOUR CLOTHES...

WHAT'S WRONG WITH YOU ALL OF A SUDDEN?

WE DON'T HAVE TIME FOR THIS. WE HAVE TO HURRY TO THE AIRPORT.

NO, BUT I SHOULD BRING SOME CHANGE OF CLOTHES...

JUST BUY THEM WHEN YOU ARRIVE.

LET'S GET UP. QUICKLY!

ALL RIGHT, ALL RIGHT. I GUESS I CAN'T EVEN DIE COMFORTABLY IN MY OWN HOUSE NOW.

MOM, I'M SORRY. BUT JUST DO AS I SAY FOR NOW.

PLEASE...

OKAY?

238

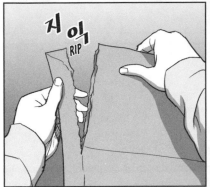

지 의
RIP

Issue No. 24

Future
Religion

"I heard the angel's prophecy"
Jinsoo Jung's interview

Jinsoo Jung testifies to his experiences in the interviewer's office

Publisher's Side

Publisher Jungchil Kim,
Doctor of Religion

I've worked diligently on it.

In this issue, I would like to present the direction and influence of religion in the new era through the testimonies of people who have come face to face with a spiritual being.

부아아앙
VROOM

244

WE WON'T LET YOU! WHY ARE YOU TRYING TO GO INTO THE CHAIRMAN'S HOUSE?!

YOU'RE PLAN-NING SOME-THING AGAIN, AREN'T YOU?

...

REP...

I'M GOING TO REPENT...

WHAT...?

...?

WHOOSH

WH...WHAT...

THE NUMBER YOU HAVE DIALED IS NOT AVAILABLE...

WHY AREN'T YOU PICKING UP?!

MOM, I'LL BE RIGHT BACK.

LOCK THE DOOR AND JUST STAY PUT.

HELLO? ATTORNEY PARK.

YOU REMEMBER THE ENVELOPE THAT I GOT YESTERDAY, RIGHT? DO YOU KNOW WHAT IT WAS ABOUT?

IT WAS A RELIGIOUS MAGAZINE THAT HAD AN INTERVIEW WITH JINSOO JUNG EIGHTEEN YEARS AGO!

ANY GUESSES ON WHAT THE INTERVIEW WAS ABOUT?

JINSOO JUNG ALSO HEARD A PROPHECY TWENTY YEARS AGO. JUST LIKE HOW JEONGJA PARK DID.

THE PROPHECY OF GOING TO HELL.

HE KNEW HE WAS GOING TO SUFFER THE SAME FATE.

AND HE STILL DID IT!

HYEJIN...

LET'S STOP NOW.

STOP? STOP WHA...

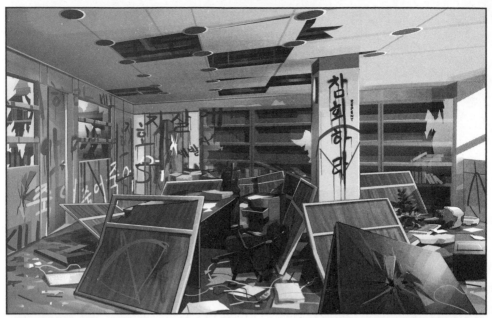

THIS WINDOW WON'T...

WOW!!

ATTORNEY PARK...THE OFFICE...

HEY, HYEJIN...I'M SO SCARED...

I QUIT...YOU SHOULD STOP IT TOO...

AND RUN AWAY...

AS FAR AS YOU CAN...

으으으으아아아아
ㅎㅎㅎㅎ

Mom
010-0000-0000

HOLD ON.
I'LL CALL
YOU BACK.

YEAH,
MOM.

MOM?

CRACK

BANG

BANG

AAKK!!!
OUCH!!

YOU
CRAZY...

CRAZY
GRANNY!!

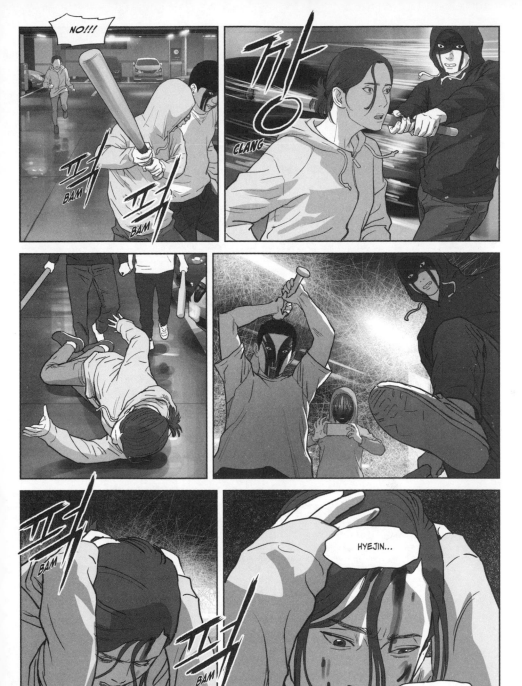

255

HYEJIN...

BAM

BAM

MOM!!
MOOOMMM!!!

HERE.

YOUR
TURN.

YOU...
YOU CRAZY
BASTARDS...
WHO'S CALLING
WHO CRAZY...

CLANG

MOM!!!

258

CRACK

HEY, SUNG HO!!!

SUNG HO JIN!!!

WHAP

SUNG HO!!!

SUNG HO...

I HAVE AN
EMERGENCY
PATIENT!!

PLEASE...
HURRY...

SHE'S...SIXTY-
SEVEN YEARS
OLD, UNDERGOING
CHEMOTHERAPY...

SHE'S BEEN
SEVERELY BEATEN.
CAN YOU HURRY...?

PUT HER ON THAT EMPTY BED FOR NOW.

MOM...

MOM, YOU HAVE TO WAKE UP. PLEASE...

...HYE...JIN...

PLEASE WAIT OUTSIDE.

I'LL BRING THE DOCTOR.

COME ON! PLEASE HURRY...

OKAY, I KNOW. PLEASE WAIT OUTSIDE.

HAA...

WHO...WHO DO I CALL...?

EXCUSE ME...HOW'S THE PATIENT I BROUGHT IN DOING?

MOM...!

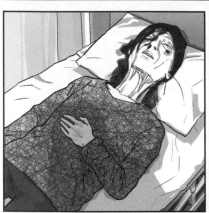

MOM...

265

HUH...?

H...HEY...

TH...THAT MAN IS TRYING TO HARM THE CHAIRMAN!

THWAK

YOU SHAMELESS PERSON!

PUT THAT GUN DOWN!

HOW DARE YOU RAISE A GUN?

...!!!!!

BAM

WHOOSH

POW

268

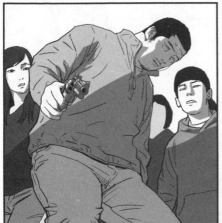
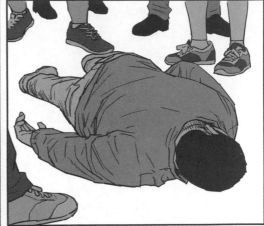

GUN! GET THE GUN FIRST!

DO WE HAVE ANYTHING TO TIE HIM UP?

CONTACT NEW TRUTH SOCIETY!

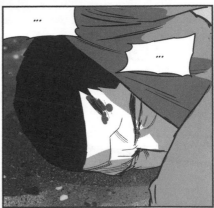

...

...

RIIINNGG

AAAAARRRRGGGHHH!!!!

JINSOO JUNG, YOU FUCKING SHIT!!!

WHERE IS MY SON?!

JI...JINSOO JUNG?

CHAIRMAN?

270

VROOOM

JINSOO JUNG!! WHERE ARE YOU?

YOU'VE BEEN THROUGH A LOT BECAUSE OF ME.

I'LL SEND YOU AN ADDRESS AFTER I HANG UP.

IF YOU WANT TO MEET SUNG HO, GO THERE.

TURN LEFT AND AFTER 30 METERS, TURN RIGHT.

YOUR DESTINATION IS 500 METERS AWAY.

부응
VROOM

JUNG HWA
ORPHANAGE

똑똑똑
KNOCK
KNOCK KNOCK

똑똑똑
KNOCK
KNOCK KNOCK

DR. JUNGCHIL KIM?

I'M HYEJIN MIN, I CALLED.

OH, YES...PLEASE COME IN.

I'VE BEEN WAITING.

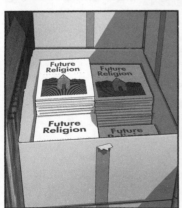

Future Religion

Future Religion

Future Religion

Future Religion

SALVATION

HISTORY OF HERESY

A SPIRITUAL LIFE

AFTER DEATH

PEOPLE WHO RETURNED FROM DEATH

NEAR-DEATH EXPERIENCE

EVIDENCE OF GOD

TRANSCENDENT

YOU CAN TAKE A SEAT OVER THERE.

SO, WHAT BRINGS YOU HERE?

275

DO YOU REMEMBER INTERVIEWING A MAN NAMED JINSOO JUNG FOR THIS MAGAZINE, EIGHTEEN YEARS AGO?

OF COURSE I DO. HE'S THE TALK OF THE TOWN RIGHT NOW IN KOREA...

DO YOU HAPPEN TO HAVE AN ORIGINAL DOCUMENT OF THIS INTERVIEW?

OH... GIVE ME A SECOND.

I THINK I HAVE THE RECORDING SOMEWHERE.

JINSOO JUNG...JINSOO JUNG...

AHA, FOUND IT.

딸깍
CLICK

HELLO, JINSOO JUNG.

YES, HELLO.

I SOUNDED SO YOUNG BACK THEN...

YOU SAID YOU HEARD A PROPHECY FROM GOD?

WELL....I'M NOT SURE IF THAT WAS GOD...

IT WAS DEFINITELY SOMETHING TERRIFYING.

SUNG HO!!

DON'T MOVE!!

HELLO, DETECTIVE.

WHERE'S SUNG HO?!

SUNG HO...

I'LL TELL YOU WHERE SUNG HO IS IF YOU LISTEN TO MY STORY.

THAT'S WHEN I FIRST SAW IT.

IT SAID TO ME...

JINSOO JUNG. TWENTY YEARS FROM NOW, ON THIS DAY AT 8:30 P.M.

YOU ARE GOING TO HELL.

IT'S A DREAM...IT MUST BE...

I TRIED MY BEST TO BELIEVE THAT WAS THE CASE...

HA HA...

YOU PROBABLY DON'T KNOW BECAUSE YOU'VE NEVER BEEN THROUGH IT, BUT...

...IT'S NOT THE KIND OF EXPERIENCE THAT YOU CAN DENY IN THAT WAY.

SO, I FRANTICALLY STARTED LOOKING FOR SIMILAR CASES.

AT FIRST, I SEARCHED IN HOPES OF IT NOT BEING TRUE...

THEN I SEARCHED TO FIND AT LEAST ONE CASE OF EXCEPTION.

DOCTOR. DO YOU THINK YOU CAN GIVE ME THE RECORDING?

HMMM... LET'S SEE...

딸깍
CLICK

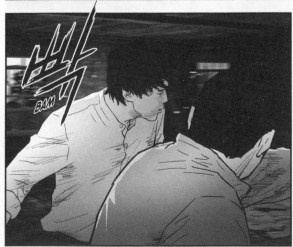

DETECTIVE, I'M ASKING YOU TO LISTEN TO ME.

WE DON'T HAVE TIME FOR THIS.

WHAT WAS YOUR SIN, YOU ASK?

YOU WERE PROBABLY INNOCENT.

OR YOU STOLE A COUPLE OF PENCILS FROM A STORE, AT WORST.

WHY DO YOU THINK THAT?

HOW CAN YOU THINK A PERSON WHO'S BEEN CHOSEN TO BE SENT TO HELL...IS INNOCENT?

BECAUSE YOU DIDN'T QUESTION HER SIN PROPERLY.

IF YOU WERE SURE THAT A LEGITIMATE SIN IS NEEDED TO BE SENT TO HELL, YOU WOULD HAVE BEEN MORE PERSISTENT.

WOW... POLICE ARE REALLY SOMETHING...

HOWEVER...

I DIDN'T EVEN STEAL A SINGLE PENCIL.

NEVER LIED...

NEVER HURT ANYONE...

I REALLY DIDN'T DO ANYTHING.

THAT'S RIGHT.

THERE'S NO WAY GOD WOULD PUNISH PEOPLE RANDOMLY.

BUT...

THAT'S THE TRUTH.

IT'S TRUE THAT THERE WERE HORRIBLE SINNERS IN THE FIRST COUPLE OF CASES I COLLECTED.

SOME MIGHT'VE NOT BEEN BRUTAL CRIMINALS, BUT THEY WERE DEFINITELY BAD PEOPLE NONETHELESS.

BUT AS CASES STARTED PILING UP, NORMAL PEOPLE...

...EVEN EXTREMELY GOOD PEOPLE STARTED RECEIVING THE NOTICE.

NO MATTER HOW MUCH I LOOKED INTO IT...NO PATTERN...

...OR INTENT COULD BE FOUND.

SOME KIND OF TRANSCENDENTAL BEING...

GOD IS... JUST MESSING WITH US.

DO YOU THINK PEOPLE WILL ACCEPT THAT?

HOW CAN MAN ENDURE SUCH GRAND NONSENSE?!

MANKIND ISN'T CAPABLE OF THAT!

HUMAN BEINGS NEED MEANING.

FAITH THAT THIS BIZARRE PHENOMENON IS GOD'S INTENTION TO MAKE THE WORLD A BETTER PLACE.

IS THAT WHY YOU DISGUISED IT AS A DEMONSTRATION AND MURDERED HIM?

TO GIVE MEANING TO GOD'S PRANK?!

EVEN THEN! WHY DID YOU BRING MY SON INTO THIS?

HONESTLY, I COULD'VE DONE IT ALONE...

BUT THEN YOU SAID SOMETHING VERY INTERESTING.

ABOUT BELIEVING IN HUMAN AUTONOMY...

BUT...BEING NICE OUT OF FEAR OF BEING RIPPED APART TO DEATH...

CAN YOU REALLY CALL THAT RIGHTEOUSNESS?

IF IT'S NOT FEAR, THEN WHAT MAKES HUMANS REPENT FOR THEIR SINS?

HAVE YOU SEEN ANYTHING LIKE IT?

IF WHAT YOU SAY IS TRUE, THEN THAT GOD YOU'RE SPEAKING OF DOESN'T BELIEVE IN HUMAN AUTONOMY.

SO...YOU LEFT IT UP TO SUNG HO'S AUTONOMY?

NO...NO...

I'M LEAVING IT UP TO YOUR AUTONOMY.

AFTER RECEIVING THE NOTICE...EVERY MOMENT, EVERY BREATH I TOOK, I WAS CRUSHED WITH FEAR.

HA HA... TWENTY YEARS... AS MANY AS TWENTY YEARS...

THAT'S WAY TOO LONG.

A FEAR THAT ONLY YOU IN THIS WORLD KNOW... ISN'T IT HORRIBLE?

IS THIS A SIN? IS THAT A SIN?

I COULDN'T GET MYSELF TO STAY INDIFFERENT EVEN FOR A SECOND.

INDIFFERENCE.

BEING NONCHALANT.

PEOPLE DON'T REALIZE HOW GREAT OF A BLESSING THAT IS.

WHEN I WAS SHOVED BY FEAR AT THE SUBWAY TRACKS...

WHEN I JUMPED INTO THE FIRE...

YOU COULD JUST STAND IN ADMIRATION.

OF COURSE, I'LL DO THAT.

HA HA...IS HIDING THE FACT ENOUGH?

I'LL POWDER AND PAINT HIM IN GOLD. I'M GOING TO RAISE HIM UP.

EXALTING OTHERS IS A SURE WAY TO EXALT YOURSELF--THAT'S WHAT THEY SAY, RIGHT?

BUT THIS GUY SAYS HE WANTS TO SEE SOME SINCERITY...

HE PUT CONDITIONS ON THE DEAL...

HE WANTS ME TO KILL YOU.

CLICK

ANYWAY, IT WAS GREAT MEETING YOU, ATTORNEY HYEJIN MIN.

CLUNK

I'M AFRAID I WON'T BE SEEING YOU AGAIN.

VROOM

VROOM

AAAAAHHHHK!!!!!!

THERE'S REALLY NOT MUCH TIME LEFT.

DETECTIVE KYUNG HOON JIN.

OUR DEAR SUNG HO SHOULD BE WAITING FOR HIS DAD BACK AT HOME.

I'LL GIVE YOU TWO OPTIONS.

THOSE THINGS ARE GOING TO COME KILL ME ANY MOMENT NOW.

IF YOU SHOOT A VIDEO AND REVEAL IT TO THE PUBLIC, PEOPLE WILL BE THROWN INTO GREAT CONFUSION.

THEN GO BACK HOME AND ARREST YOUR SON.

IF YOU DO THAT, YOU MIGHT BE ABLE TO EXTEND YOUR LIFE A LITTLE LONGER.

IF THAT'S NOT IT, THEN REMAIN SILENT ABOUT MY DEATH.

AND YOU AND SUNG HO CAN ENJOY THE WORLD THAT I'VE PREPARED.

THUMP...

THEY'RE
HERE...

THUMP

THUMP

THUMP

THUMP

THUMP

DRR

DAD?

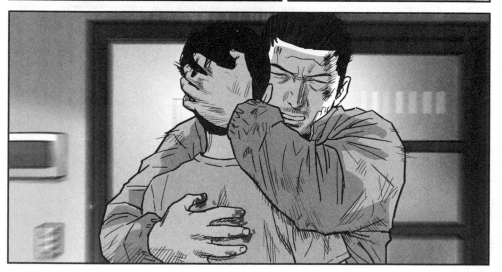

Continue to the second world of hell.

"Welcome . . . to the New World."
A manmade hell.

CHAIRMAN OF NEW TRUTH SOCIETY, JINSOO JUNG
"Why do people sin? . . . People sin because they want to sin. By denying that fact, human beings lost humiliation, a sense of guilt, atonement, repentance . . . God is showing us an image of hell very bluntly. God's intentions are very clear. You have to be more righteous."

DETECTIVE KYUNG HOON JIN
"Cops catch criminals. Whether they killed a bad guy or an innocent person . . . whether they killed to save the world or just to have fun . . . we catch whoever committed a murder. That's our job."

ATTORNEY HYEJIN MIN
"I don't even know what's happening. Feels like the world I once knew is fading away."

ARROWHEAD LEADER
"We have someone who received the notice from hell in our country!! That's not all!! What's even more shocking is that — they are going to live broadcast the sinner going to hell!! Arrowhead! Arrowhead! How has my family been? How much did you have to suffer among the blind? But!! In two days, every citizen, every human being on Earth, will hear us!! All of your hardships were a part of the preparation for this very moment!"

JEONGJA PARK
"Chairman . . . I don't care what it is . . . I don't care what you label my crime as . . . Just anything . . . I'm so fortunate. I was never able to do anything as a mother. This is my lucky chance. Please help so that my kids can live well in a place where no one can find them. I beg you."

CREATOR BIOGRAPHIES

YEON SANG-HO

Animation director, film director, and producer. Graduated from Sangmyung University with a degree in western painting. He directed the animated films *The King of Pigs, The Fake, Seoul Station,* and more. In 2012, Yeon Sang-ho received an invitation to the 65th Cannes Film Festival Directors' Fortnight. Additionally, he was invited to the midnight screening at the 69th Cannes Film Festival with *Train to Busan.* With *Train to Busan* attracting ten million viewers, Yeon Sang-ho further broadened his boundaries as a live-action film director. In 2020, *Peninsula* was chosen to be shown in the Official Selection of the 73rd Cannes Film Festival. Yeon Sang-ho is the only director invited to Cannes for both live-action and animated films. Yeon Sang-ho was chosen by Cannes in succession with *Train to Busan* and *Peninsula,* both of which share the same universe. In charge of the story of *The Hellbound* and writing the screenplay of the TVN drama *The Cursed,* Yeon Sang-ho is currently engaged in various projects.

CHOI GYU-SEOK

Cartoonist. Graduated from Sangmyung University with a degree in cartooning and animation. He debuted in 1998 in Seoul Cultural Publisher's Rookie Cartoon Contest. Some of his representative works include *A Sad Homage to Dinosaur Dooly, Wetlands Ecology Report, Natives of Republic of Korea, 100C, A Little Vague to Cry, A Story That Doesn't Exist Now,* and *Awl.* Choi Gyu-seok's works have been translated and published in Europe, Japan, and the United States. He has won numerous awards, including an award in the Short Animation category in the Seoul International Cartoon and Animation Festival, the excellence award in the Korean Comic Awards, a grand prize in the Child and Youth Category for the Korea Book Awards, and Today's Our Manhwa Award. He also won two grand prizes at the Bucheon Comics Awards in 2011 and 2018, for *A Little Vague to Cry* and *Awl,* respectively.

VOLUME 2—COMING MAY 2022!

president and publisher
MIKE RICHARDSON

editor
JUDY KHUU

designer
BRENNAN THOME

assistant editor
ROSE WEITZ

digital art technicians
JOSIE CHRISTENSEN AND **BETSY MILLER**

Special thanks to Kari Torson at Dark Horse Comics.

Neil Hankerson EXECUTIVE VICE PRESIDENT | Tom Weddle CHIEF FINANCIAL OFFICER | Dale LaFountain CHIEF INFORMATION OFFICER | Tim Wiesch VICE PRESIDENT OF LICENSING | Matt Parkinson VICE PRESIDENT OF MARKETING | Vanessa Todd-Holmes VICE PRESIDENT OF PRODUCTION AND SCHEDULING | Mark Bernardi VICE PRESIDENT OF BOOK TRADE AND DIGITAL SALES | Randy Lahrman VICE PRESIDENT OF PRODUCT DEVELOPMENT | Ken Lizzi GENERAL COUNSEL | Dave Marshall EDITOR IN CHIEF | Davey Estrada EDITORIAL DIRECTOR | Chris Warner SENIOR BOOKS EDITOR | Cary Grazzini DIRECTOR OF SPECIALTY PROJECTS | Lia Ribacchi ART DIRECTOR | Matt Dryer DIRECTOR OF DIGITAL ART AND PREPRESS | Michael Gombos SENIOR DIRECTOR OF LICENSED PUBLICATIONS | Kari Yadro DIRECTOR OF CUSTOM PROGRAMS | Kari Torson DIRECTOR OF INTERNATIONAL LICENSING

THE HELLBOUND VOLUME 1

Published by Dark Horse Books | A division of Dark Horse Comics LLC | 10956 SE Main Street | Milwaukie, OR 97222

DarkHorse.com | To find a comics shop in your area, visit comicshoplocator.com

Library of Congress Cataloging-in-Publication Data
Names: Sang-Ho, Yeon, writer. | Gyu-Seok, Choi, artist. | Lim, Danny,
    translator. | Heisler, Michael, letterer.
Title: The hellbound / writer, Yeon Sang-Ho ; artist, Choi Gyu-Seok ;
    letters, Michael Heisler ; translator, Danny Lim.
Other titles: Hell. English
Description: Milwaukie, OR : Dark Horse Books, 2021-
Identifiers: LCCN 2021017722 | ISBN 9781506726885 (v. 1 ; trade paperback)
Subjects: LCSH: Graphic novels.
Classification: LCC PN6790.K63 S36413 2021 | DDC 741.5/95195--dc23
LC record available at https://lccn.loc.gov/2021017722

First English-language edition: November 2021
ISBN 978-1-50672-688-5

1 3 5 7 9 10 8 6 4 2
Printed in the United States of America